Brilliant guides

What you need to know and how to do it

When you're working on your computer and come up against a problem that you're unsure how to solve, or want to accomplish something in an application that you aren't sure how to do, where do you look? Manuals and traditional training guides are usually too big and unwieldy and are intended to be used as end-to-end training resources, making it hard to get to the info you need right away without having to wade through pages of background information that you just don't need at that moment – and helplines are rarely that helpful!

Brilliant guides have been developed to allow you to find the info you need easily and without fuss and guide you through the task using a highly visual, step-by-step approach – providing exactly what you need to know when you need it!

Brilliant guides provide the quick easy-to-access information that you need, using a table of contents and troubleshooting guide to help you find exactly what you need to know, and then presenting each task in a visual manner. Numbered steps guide you through each task or problem, using numerous screenshots to illustrate each step. Added features include 'See also...' boxes that point you to related tasks and information in the book, while 'Did you know?...' sections alert you to relevant expert tips, tricks and advice to further expand your skills and knowledge.

In addition to covering all major office PC applications, and related computing subjects, the *Brilliant* series also contains titles that will help you in every aspect of your working life, such as writing the perfect CV, answering the toughest interview questions and moving on in your career.

Brilliant guides are the light at the end of the tunnel when you are faced with any minor or major task.

Author's dedications

This book is dedicated to my dear Mom. The encouragement, belief and 'stick with it' attitude you handed down to me has worked wonders in pursuing the lofty goals of one who walks a different path. That make it on your own, on your terms approach is running through our family line, and I enjoy seeing it work its way down right into my son's psyche as well. No mention of Mom in a computer book would be complete without also honoring my stepfather, Rick. He was into computers since the days when an IBM mainframe was all the rage. Mom and Rick suggested I take a look into computers, well before it was fashionable to do so. That advice was literally life changing.

Author's acknowledgements

With great pleasure I thank the team at Prentice Hall/Pearson. Katy Robinson and Steve Temblett kept patient as I tested and tweaked JavaScript routines to run in as many browsers as possible. Cross-browser issues are the bane of client-side web development. Behind the scenes a cast of publishing professionals will produce a Brilliant book from a manuscript. This is a joint effort that many will participate in without much credit, so I offer my thanks to all involved, and know that your contributions are vital and appreciated.

My continued thanks to Neil Salkind and the StudioB team. It is an honor to work with all of you.

About the author

After a decade of business management, Ken switched to writing software in the early 1990s. He became involved with website development shortly after – just as the Internet was becoming known and widely used. Over the years Ken has worked in many industries and positions – as a database developer and DBA, as a project manager and trainer, and of course as a rolled-up sleeves, grinding out the code programmer.

Over the past few years Ken has been devoted primarily to web development and design, working on projects for every concern – from mom-and-pop shops to huge intranet applications for Fortune 500 companies. Embracing the new Web 2.0 fad, Ken is busy setting up social network sites. Between writing, developing and daily life obligations, he occasionally gets away to go hiking, and to follow his musical pursuits. Ken lives in Pennsylvania, in the United States – with his wife, son, cats, and assorted lizards and amphibians. Visit Ken at www.kenbluttman.com.

Contents

Introduction

Welcome to *Brilliant JavaScript*, a visual quick reference book that provides an introduction to programming with THE scripting language of the Web, JavaScript. It will give you a solid grounding on how to use basic Javascript programming to improve the functionality and design of your webpages, validate forms, detect browsers, create cookies, and much more – a complete reference for the beginner and intermediate user.

Find what you need to know – when you need it

You don't have to read this book in any particular order. We've designed the book so that you can jump in, get the information you need, and jump out. To find the information that you need, just look up the task in the table of contents or Troubleshooting guide, and turn to the page listed. Read the task introduction, follow the step-by-step instructions along with the illustration, and you're done.

How this book works

Each task is presented with step-by-step instructions in one column and screen illustrations in the other. This arrangement lets you focus on a single task without having to turn the pages too often.

Step-by-step instructions

This book provides concise step-by-step instructions that show you how to accomplish a task. Each set of instructions includes illustrations that directly correspond to the easy-to-read steps. Eye-catching text features provide additional helpful information in bite-sized chunks to help you work more efficiently or to teach you more in-depth information. The 'For your information' features provide tips and techniques to help you work smarter, while the 'See also' cross-references lead you to other parts of the book containing related information about the task. Essential information is highlighted in 'Important' boxes that will ensure you don't miss any vital suggestions and advice.

Troubleshooting guide

This book offers quick and easy ways to diagnose and solve common problems that you might encounter, using the Troubleshooting guide. The problems are grouped into categories that are presented alphabetically.

Spelling

We have used UK spelling conventions throughout this book. You may therefore notice some inconsistencies between the text and the software on your computer, which is likely to have been developed in the US. We have, however adopted US spelling for the words 'disk' and 'program', as these are commonly accepted throughout the world.

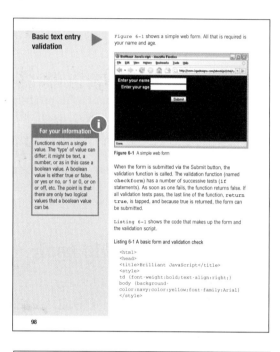

Getting started with JavaScript

Introduction

JavaScript is a client-side technology. This means that any JavaScript routines (or scripts as they may be called) run within your browser. JavaScript does not run on the web server. With this in mind JavaScript is the primary tool to perform tasks that need to take place locally in your browser. The most common of these are to provide animation on the web page, and to validate data entered into the web page.

There are of course many other uses for JavaScript and many will be showcased in this book. However, first things first. In this chapter you will learn what the most basic but necessary elements are of a script. Also, this chapter discusses the various places where a script can be placed within the HTML code. Rounding out the chapter are tasks that show how two major programming concerns – decision making and sequential processing (or looping) – are handled in JavaScript.

What you'll do

Learn the basic elements of a script

Place a script in the head section of an HTML page

Use inline scripting

Link to an external JavaScript file

Learn how conditional programming works in JavaScript

Learn how loops are used in JavaScript

Use basic debugging techniques

Why JavaScript is so important?

The process of having a web page show up in a browser involves having information sent from a web server into the browser. The type of data can be comprised of many things. All web pages have HTML code, but they can also include graphics, small application-based features such as a Flash movie, widgets and more.

Many of the activities that take place on a web page in your browser depend on JavaScript to function. In other words, JavaScript can play the part of helping another type of technology to work. A common example is using JavaScript to test which browser you are using and make adjustments on how information is displayed.

JavaScript is also vital when information is sent back to the web server from your browser. Client-side validation is a major JavaScript speciality. JavaScript can be used to make sure all required form fields are filled in and that they are filled in correctly. When this type of validation fails, the sending of data back to the server is avoided, preserving bandwidth and not placing any incorrect data on the server.

A script can only run when the browser recognises a script for what it is. The `<script>` and `</script>` HTML tags identify a script block. Using these tags is necessary to instruct the browser where to start and stop the interpretation of the JavaScript code. It is perfectly acceptable to have multiple script blocks within a single page of HTML code. This actually provides a useful way to have scripts run within different areas of a web page. Scripts can be inserted into the head or body sections of a web page. These options are discussed later in the chapter.

By making use of functions in JavaScript you can control when a script will run; that is, you can override a script from running when a page loads into the browser. This approach will be showcased many times throughout the book.

Listing 1-1 shows a basic HTML web page with a JavaScript script.

Listing 1-1 A basic JavaScript

```html
<html>
<head>
<title>Brilliant JavaScript</title>
<style>
body {font-family:arial,helvetica,sans-
serif;font-weight:bold;background-
color:#ffffcc}
</style>
<script type="text/javascript">
   alert ("I am a basic javascript script,
and I'm loving it!");
</script>
</head>
<body>
</body>
</html>
```

Writing a basic script

Jargon buster

A **function** is a discrete programming routine. Functions are called to run when needed. A perfect example is when you click a submit button to process an online form. Typically a validation routine will run in this case, upon the action of clicking the button.

Important

The HTML `<script>` `</script>` tag set can contain other scripting languages, such as VBScript. But by and large JavaScript is the de facto client-based scripting language.

Writing a basic script (cont.)

The majority of the code in Listing 1-1 is HTML. The basic JavaScript routine within it is this:

```
<script type="text/javascript">
  alert ("I am a basic javascript script,
  and I'm loving it!");
</script>
```

The least required valid JavaScript exists in these three short lines. The opening `script` tag specifies the type of script to be run. In this case, JavaScript of course! The syntax for specifying JavaScript is contained in the `type` attribute, as in `type="text/javascript"`. This `type` attribute is included within the opening `script` tag.

The `alert` command tells the browser to display a popup message window, the text of the window being what is specified with the alert command. Finally the script closes with the ending script tag (`</script>`). Figure 1-1 shows the windowed message that appears when the page is loaded.

Figure 1-1 A message from a script

Here are the steps to take to run this wonderful JavaScript example:

1. Create a new HTML web page, or open an existing one.

2. In the head section, enter the three specific JavaScript code lines – the beginning and ending script tags, and the alert statement in the middle line.

3. Save the HTML file and open it in your browser, or refresh your browser if the page is already open.

Important !

JavaScript is notorious for being a picky, pesky language. The most innocent of syntax errors will cause all the JavaScript to fail. If the example did not produce the message box, check closely that all spelling is correct, including that the case treatment is the same (upper case, lower case). Also look for any missing punctuation, such as a missing quote mark or parenthesis, or a missing semicolon on the end of the middle line.

Placing your script in the head section

Although a script can be placed in the head or the body of a web page, the predominant place is the head. From the perspective of organisation this makes sense, particularly for script routines that include functions. The nature of a function is to be called into action from another part of the page, so keeping the functions in the head keeps them together for easy review.

A further aspect of script in the head placement is the sequence and positioning of the output from a script. Placing a script in the body fixes the script to run and produce any visible output exactly where it sits in the body HTML. In contrast JavaScript routines placed in the head run as the page is loaded. This provides efficiencies for setting up images in the page, or running any processing that needs to occur upon the page being ready in the browser.

Listing 1-2 shows the source of an HTML page. The JavaScript block is in the head.

Listing 1-2 A block of JavaScript is in the head section of the web page

```
<html>
<head>
<title>Brilliant JavaScript</title>
<style>
body {font-family:arial,helvetica,sans-
serif;font-weight:bold;background-
color:#ffffcc}
</style>
<script type="text/javascript">
   document.write ("Good Afternoon!");
</script>
</head>
<body>
<br />
<br />
Whether 'tis nobler in the mind to suffer
The slings and arrows of outrageous fortune,
Or to take arms against a sea of troubles
</body>
</html>
```

The set of code in Listing 1-2 presents text in the browser. 'Good Afternoon!' is written to the browser by the JavaScript in the head section. The quote from Shakespeare's *Hamlet* is plain text rendered via normal HTML processing.

Referring to Figure 1-2:

1. The JavaScript block in the head uses the `document.write` action to show the text in the browser.

2. The text in the body appears in accordance with where it is placed within the HTML portion of the page.

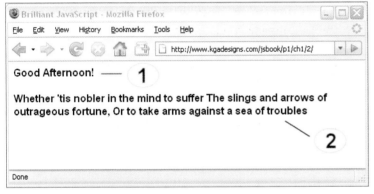

Figure 1-2 Writing text from a JavaScript routine

Placing JavaScript in the web page body

Placing JavaScript in the body of a web page has the effect of the JavaScript running serially where it sits in the body. In other words a JavaScript routine at the beginning of the body section will run prior to another JavaScript routine further down the page.

Listing 1-3 shows the code of a web page in which text is written to the browser in this sequence:

1. 'Good morning!' is written from the first JavaScript routine.

2. 'If music be the food of love, play on' is just plain text within the code and appears as such.

3. 'I must be going now!' is written from a second JavaScript routine.

Listing 1-3 Multiple JavaScript routines in the document body

```
<html>
<head>
<title>Brilliant JavaScript</title>
<style>
body {font-family:arial,helvetica,sans-
serif;font-weight:bold;background-
color:#ffffcc}
</style>
</head>
<body>
<script type="text/javascript">
   document.write ("Good morning!");
</script>
<br /><br /><br />
If music be the food of love, play on
<br /><br /><br />
<script type="text/javascript">
   document.write ("I must be going now!");
</script>
</body>
</html>
```

Figure 1-3 shows the output of the code in Listing 1-3. The three textual outputs referenced above are indicated in Figure 1-3. The placement of the text follows the placement of the JavaScript routines within the code.

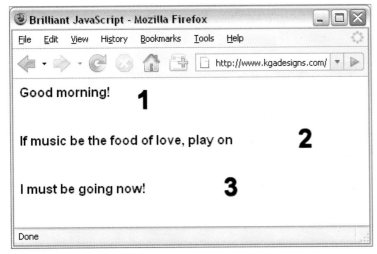

Figure 1-3 A mix of JavaScript written text and plain text

Using an external JavaScript file

A powerful technique that can be used when coding web pages is to link to external code files. Of the various types of files that can be linked, JavaScript is a major one. CSS (cascading style sheet) files are also often linked.

The great advantage of using external files is this: suppose you have several web pages that all share common elements such as an address block or logo, or a navigation bar or menu. If a change is required to a common element, having that element linked into each page allows you to change it in one place – in the external file. That sure beats having to make the change on each individual page. At first the concept of linking in files might be confusing, but the time and effort spent using this approach quickly becomes apparent. If coding web pages is your cup of tea, then you will end up using external files. Really, you will.

So how does this work? Listing 1-4 shows the code of an HTML page. Two linked files are referenced, in these two lines:

```
<script type="text/javascript"
src="makedate.js"></script>
<script type="text/javascript"
src="writetext.js"></script>
```

Listing 1-4 shows the full code of the HTML page. Listing 1-5 shows the code contained in **makedate.js**, and Listing 1-6 shows the code contained in **writetext.js**.

Listing 1-4 A web page with references to external JavaScript files

```
<html>
<head>
<title>Brilliant JavaScript</title>
<style>
body {font-family:arial,helvetica,sans-
serif;font-weight:bold;background-
color:#ffffcc}
</style>
<script type="text/javascript"
src="makedate.js"></script>
```

For your information

The syntax creates the link. Simply use the `src=` construct along with the external file name. If necessary a path and file name can be used to point to the external file. In this example only filenames are supplied, therefore the files must be in the same directory with the web page.

```
<script type="text/javascript"
src="writetext.js"></script>
</head>
<body>
<br /><br /><br />
A horse! A horse! My kingdom for a horse!
<br /><br /><br />
<form>
<input type="button" value="Click me"
onclick="writetext()" />
</form>
<div id="placeonpage"></div>
</body>
</html>
```

Listing 1-5 The contents of the `makedate.js` file

```
var d=new Date();
var month=new Array(12);
month[0]="1";
month[1]="2";
month[2]="3";
month[3]="4";
month[4]="5";
month[5]="6";
month[6]="7";
month[7]="8";
month[8]="9";
month[9]="10";
month[10]="11";
month[11]="12";
document.write(month[d.getMonth()] + "/" +
d.getDate() + "/" + d.getFullYear());
```

Listing 1-6 The contents of the `writetext.js` file

```
function writetext() {
  var placeonpage=document.getElementById
  ("placeonpage");
placeonpage.innerHTML="A Pie! A Pie! My
kingdom for a pie!";
}
```

Using an external JavaScript file (cont.)

In this example a few key things occur. When the page loads, the JavaScript code contained in the `makedate.js` file runs. As seen in Listing 1-5, the contents of `makedate.js` are JavaScript, of course, but none of the code is contained in a function. Therefore the code runs upon the loading of the page in the browser. Figure 1-4 shows how the page looks when it loads.

Figure 1-4 The web page displays the output from the external `makedate.js` file

The `writetext.js` does not run without an intervening action – namely clicking a button to make the code run. As seen in Figure 1-4, the web page loads with a button. The date at the top of the page was written by the script in the `makedate.js` file, and the text is just plain text from the web page proper. Clicking the button runs the script in the `writetext.js` file. As shown in Listing 1-6, `writetext.js` holds a JavaScript function. A function runs when some action calls it. In this case the button click is the action. The line of code that displays the button also includes the call to the external file:

```
<input type="button" value="Click me"
onclick="writetext()" />
```

The `onclick` action calls the `writetext()` function. The function writes an additional line of text into the page, shown here in Figure 1-5.

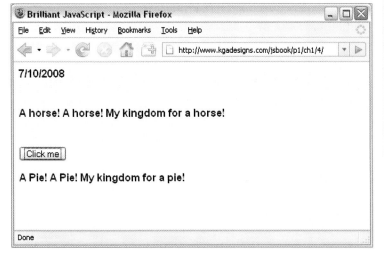

Figure 1-5 Further text appears in the page when the button is clicked

New concepts

A few key code constructs are introduced in this example, so here is a quick rundown of them:

- External JavaScript files have the `.js` extension.
- The HTML `src` tag is used to link the external files to the page.
- JavaScript contained in a function will not run until an action or event starts it.
- One way of calling a function to run is to use the `onclick` event (of a button).
- Use `getElementById` to place text at a specific location (in an HTML `<div></div>` tag set) (see Chapter 7).

Testing a condition to determine the output

Conditional processing is a necessary tenet of programming. All programming languages contain conditional testing, basically taking one type of action or another based on the result of testing a condition. For example, if the time of day when a page is loading is in the morning then display 'Good morning'; if it is not in the morning then display a different message or take some other action.

Conditional testing can be as simple as determining if a condition is true or not (example – 10 years or greater: yes or no). Complex conditional testing tests for a number of cascading or nested conditions and takes an action when the correct result is found.

There are two methods of conditional testing to use in JavaScript. One method uses the **if** statement, along with other keywords such as **else** and **else if**. Using **if** statements can create powerful code it but can be difficult to write the code to achieve the correct intention. The other conditional testing method is the **switch** statement. The **switch** statement is easy to follow. A list of possible actions is presented, and one is taken when a condition is met.

Listing 1-7 shows code which contains both types of conditional testing. Additionally, the **if** style of testing is presented in both a simple fashion and a complex one. Altogether, then, three tests are done.

Listing 1-7 Conditional testing

```
<html>
<head>
<title>Brilliant JavaScript</title>
<style>
body {font-family:arial,helvetica,sans-
serif;font-weight:bold;background-
color:#ffffcc}
</style>
<script type="text/javascript">
var theday = new Date();
var thedayofweek = theday.getDay();
if (thedayofweek==6) {
```

```javascript
    document.write ("Today is Saturday");
} else {
    document.write ("Today is not
    Saturday");
}
document.write ("<br /><br />");
var thetime = theday.getHours();
if (thetime < 12) {
    document.write ("Good Morning!");
} else if (thetime > 11 && thetime < 18) {
    document.write ("Good Afternoon!");
} else {
    document.write ("Good Evening!");
}
document.write ("<br /><br />");
var themonth = theday.getMonth();
switch (themonth) {
    case 0:
        document.write ("The month is
        January");
        break;
    case 1:
        document.write ("The month is
        February");
        break;
    case 2:
        document.write ("The month is
        March");
        break;
    case 3:
        document.write ("The month is
        April");
        break;
    case 4:
        document.write ("The month is May");
        break;
    case 5:
        document.write ("The month is
        June");
        break;
    case 6:
        document.write ("The month is
        July");
        break;
```

```
        case 7:
            document.write ("The month is
            August");
            break;
        case 8:
            document.write ("The month is
            September");
            break;
        case 9:
            document.write ("The month is
            October");
            break;
        case 10:
            document.write ("The month is
            November");
            break;
        case 11:
            document.write ("The month is
            December");
            break;
        default:
            document.write ("Can't determine the
            month");
    }
    </script>
    </head>
    <body>
    </body>
    </html>
```

In Listing 1-7 the first test is for a simple yes or no condition: is it Saturday?:

```
if (thedayofweek==6) {
    document.write ("Today is Saturday");
} else {
    document.write ("Today is not Saturday");
}
```

The second test extends the simple test to check for three possible outcomes:

```
if (thetime < 12) {
   document.write ("Good Morning!");
} else if (thetime > 11 && thetime < 18) {
   document.write ("Good Afternoon!");
} else {
   document.write ("Good Evening!");
}
```

In Listing 1-7 the `switch` statement starts with the test `switch (themonth)` and then lists a series of possible truths. Each tested condition starts with the `case` keyword and ends with the `break` statement. At the end a last option is included using the `default` keyword to provide the action to take if none of the previous `case` blocks is true. The necessity of using `default` as a catch-all depends on what is being tested. In this example the number of the current month is being tested and all possibilities of the numeric month equivalent are present. In this example, the `default` block will never be used, but I put it there for illustration.

Figure 1-6 shows the output in my browser. Clearly, I made this screen shot not on Saturday, in the morning, and in July.

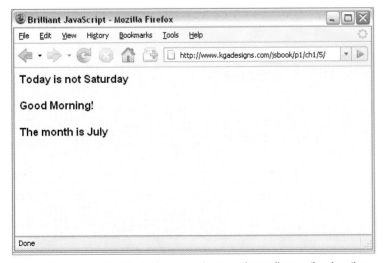

Figure 1-6 The output in the browser changes depending on the day, time and month

How to use conditional testing

■ Decide which type of testing to use: `if` or `switch`. This is a subjective decision. A good guideline is if you have more than a few possible outcomes, use the `switch` statement.

■ When using `if`, the test goes inside parentheses and an open curly brace follows right after. A closing curly brace ends the `if` block. Curly braces are also used around the `else` keyword if one is used. See the above example.

■ When using `switch` also be aware of the curly braces and that the `break` statements end with a semicolon (`break;`).

■ Multiple `if` statements can be used in either a nested or a sequential configuration. A set of sequential `if` statements is quite similar to how the `switch` statement works.

Getty loopy

In terms of syntax this is how the loops are structured:

- The `for` statement initialises a variable to a given value, a test of the variable's value is used to determine whether to keep looping, and finally the value of the variable is increased (or could be decreased if that serves the need). The `for` block looks like this:

```
for (initial variable value; test of the
variable; change of the variable's value)  {

   actions go here

}
```

- The `while` statement is structured as:

```
initialise variable

while (test of variable) {

   actions go here

increment or decrement the variable's value

}
```

- The `do while` loop is structured as:

```
initialise variable

do {

   actions go here including the increment or
   decrement of the variable

}

while (test variable)
```

Bemoan the mundane. Surely the more repetitive a process is, the more boring it is. Luckily we have computers to do the work! As with any programming language the ability to loop through code is a core feature of JavaScript. Looping is done with the `for` statement or the `while` statement, or by using what is called a `do while` loop.

There is a succinct difference between the `while` loop and the `do while` loop. The difference is where the test is performed, either at the beginning or at the end of the loop. This provides a choice on how to apply the value of the tested variable. For example, when the variable test becomes false, do no more iterations (the test is at the beginning of the loop); or complete the iteration that includes the variable making the test false (the testing is at the end of the loop). If this is confusing, well that's because it is! Whether you test at the start or at the end really doesn't matter because you can always change how the variable is being tested. The two variations of `while` looping probably exist because these variations are found in most other programming languages as well. The `for` loop is much more popular anyway. Listing 1-8 contains the code of a web page that uses the three types of loops.

Listing 1-8 A page full of looping methods

```
<html>
<head>
<title>Brilliant JavaScript</title>
<style>
body {font-family:arial,helvetica,sans-
serif;font-weight:bold;background-
color:#ffffcc}
</style>
<script type="text/javascript">
for (i=2;i<=1024;i=i*2) {
   document.write (i + " ");
}
document.write ("<br /><br />");
var i=3;
while (i<=1000) {
   document.write (i + "  
     ");
   i = i * 3;
}
document.write ("<br /><br />");
loopcount=1;
document.write("<br />12 Numbers in the
```

```
Fibonacci Sequence")
x=0;
y=1;
do {
loopcount=loopcount + 1;
z = y + x;
x=y;
y=z;
document.write("<br />" + z);
}
while (loopcount<13)
</script>
</head>
<body>
<br>
</body>
</html>
```

Taking a close look at the **for** loop, it is clear that the variable is used within the action that writes to the browser. As long as **i** is equal to or less than 1024, write the value of **i** followed by a space:

```
for (i=2;i<=1024;i=i*2) {
   document.write (i + " ");
}
```

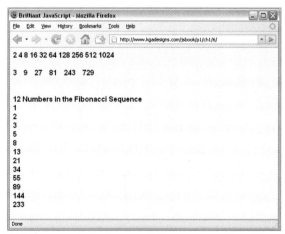

Figure 1-7 The output in the browser listing powers of 2 and 3 and the first 12 numbers in the Fibonacci sequence

The two **while** loops are used in a similar fashion. Figure 1-7 shows the how the page is output in the browser.

A loop will repeat a process either to a fixed number of iterations or until an expected condition is met. A good programming approach is to take an appropriate action when something unintended happens. For example, suppose a loop is running through a number of employee records in order to calculate their weekly pay amount. The formula calculates the hourly rate multiplied by the number of hours worked. A worker mistakenly has an entry of a negative number of hours. This is bad data. A way to handle this could be to stop processing the loop and report the error.

Listing 1-9 shows a script that calculates the weekly pay for six employees. For simplicity they all earn £20 per hour. This number is hard-coded in the script.

Listing 1-9 Using a loop to calculate employee weekly pay amounts

```
<html>
<head>
<title>Brilliant JavaScript</title>
<style>
body {font-family:arial,helvetica,sans-
serif;font-weight:bold;background-
color:#ffffcc}
</style>
<script type="text/javascript">
var employees = new Array("Aaron", "Amy",
"Bill", "Betsy", "Craig", "Cindy");
var hours = new Array(36, 32, 24, 28, -32,
24);
var count = employees.length;
for (i=0;i<count;i++) {
  week_income= hours[i] * 20;
  document.write (employees[i] + "
earned &#163;" + week_income + ".");
  document.write ("<br />");
}
</script>
</head>
<body>
</body>
</html>
```

Breaking out of a loop

For your information

This script uses arrays. These are collections of similar pieces of information. For example, the employees array contains the names of the employees. Chapter 5 is where arrays are discussed and put to use.

Breaking out of a loop (cont.)

Figure 1-8 shows the output of the script in Listing 1-9. As seen, Craig is reported to have earned –640 pounds. Craig will not be happy about that! Even more of an issue is that the employer needs to know that the process can return bad data.

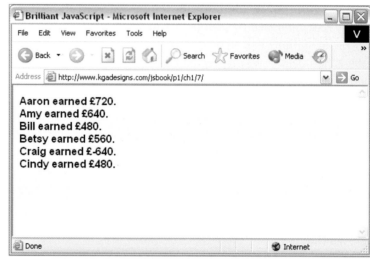

Figure 1-8 The result of calculating weekly pay

An `if` statement is now used to test for erroneous results. Within the `if` statement is a `break` statement that will force the processing to exit the loop if the condition being tested in the `if` statement is met (if the calculated amount is less than zero). Listing 1-10 is an updated version of the routine shown in Listing 1-9 with the `if` statement nested inside the loop.

Listing 1-10 Breaking out of a loop if a bad result is calculated

```
<html>
<head>
<title>Brilliant JavaScript</title>
<style>
body {font-family:arial,helvetica,sans-
serif;font-weight:bold;background-
color:#ffffcc}
</style>
<script type="text/javascript">
var employees = new Array("Aaron", "Amy",
"Bill", "Betsy", "Craig", "Cindy");
```

```
var hours = new Array(36, 32, 24, 28, -24,
24);
var count = employees.length;
for (i=0;i<count;i++) {
  week_income= hours[i] * 20;
  if (week_income<0 || isNaN(week_income))
  {
    document.write("<br />");
    document.write("Error while processing
    the salary for " + employees[i]);
    break;
  }
  document.write ( employees[i] + " earned
  &#163;" + week_income + ".<br />");
}
</script>
</head>
<body>
</body>
</html>
```

As seen in Figure 1-9 the processing catches the bad data calculation, stops looping, and writes the error information to the browser window.

Breaking out of a loop (cont.)

1

For your information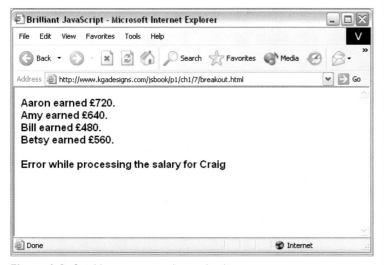

The script in Listing 1-10 contains an odd function – **isNaN** – which reads 'is not a number'.

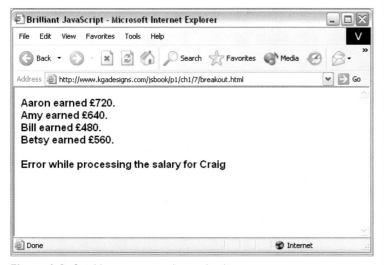

Aaron earned £720.
Amy earned £640.
Bill earned £480.
Betsy earned £560.

Error while processing the salary for Craig

Figure 1-9 Catching an error and reporting it

Debugging JavaScript

Catching logic errors and incorrect results is handled by your code. But what about syntax errors? These are errors of the coding itself, such as misspelling a keyword, leaving out a closing curly brace, and so on.

As many a JavaScript developer will testify, debugging syntax and incorrect coding structures is notoriously frustrating. Since JavaScript runs in the browser, it is within the browser that one uses any available debugging tools. Since there are many browsers available, there is no standard for a debugging platform. In this section I will show you a couple of techniques and what to expect from two different popular browsers.

First, Listing 1-11 shows a script with an error. Something is missing and your eyes may not catch it.

Listing 1-11 This script contains a syntax error

```
<script type="text/javascript">
var theday = new Date();
var dayofweek = theday.getDay();

switch (dayofweek) {
    case 0:
        dd="Sunday";
        break;
    case 1:
        dd="Monday";
        break;
    case 2:
        dd="Tuesday";
        break;
    case 3:
        dd="Wednesday";
        break;
    case 4:
        dd="Thursday";
        break;
    case 5:
        dd="Friday";
        break;
    case 6:
        dd="Saturday";
        break;
```

```
        default:
                document.write ("Can't determine
    the day of the week");
    }
    document.write(Today is " + dd);
    </script>
```

If it is not clear what is wrong, then displaying the error when
run in the browser will help, as seen in Figure 1-10.

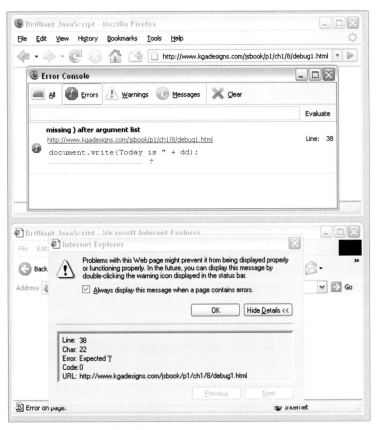

Figure 1-10 Debugging help

Figure 1-10 shows Firefox 2 on top and Internet Explorer 6 on
the bottom. On top of each browser is an error reporting
window. Each error message correctly identifies the line with
the error, which is a missing quote mark before the word
`Today` in the line:

```
document.write(Today is " + dd);
```

Debugging JavaScript (cont.)

At times you have errors that are not based on faulty syntax but rather on incorrect, yet proper, syntax. Listing 1-12 shows a portion of a validation script.

Listing 1-12 No syntax error but still does not work

```
function checkform(f) {
   if (f.elements["txtFirstName"].value.
   replace(/\s/g, "")="") {
      alert ("Please fill in your first
      name");
      f.elements["txtFirstName"].focus();
      return false;
}
      if (f.elements["txtLastName"].
      value.replace(/\s/g, "")=="") {
      alert ("Please fill in your last
      name");
      f.elements["txtLastName"].focus();
      return false;
   }
```

The code tests to see if the first name and last name entry boxes on a web page are filled in. In usage the last name validation does indeed alert (by a popup message) a person that did not fill in their last name, but the first name could be left empty and still pass the validation.

All the code checks out in terms of correct syntax. Here, then, one approach is to intersperse **alert** messages throughout the lines of code to see which ones show up. Listing 1-13 shows a modification of the code.

Listing 1-13 Using alert statements to diagnose the problem

```
function checkform(f) {
alert ("1");
   if (f.elements["txtFirstName"].value.
   replace(/\s/g, "")="") {
      alert ("Please fill in your first
      name");
```

```
        f.elements ["txtFirstName"].focus ();
   alert ("2");
        return false;
   alert ("3");
      }
   alert ("4");
     if (f.elements ["txtLastName"].value.
     replace (/\s/g, "")=="") {
        alert ("Please fill in your last name");
        f.elements ["txtLastName"].focus ();
        return false;
     }
```

Numbered `alert` statements are placed throughout the
suspected trouble area. When this example was next run, alert
1 would appear followed by alert 4. Since alert 2 and alert 3
never appeared, it was easy to conclude that the entire block of
code that tests the first name was not being used. This allowed
the focus to be on the first line of the block, and the problem
was quickly identified. For whatever reason the line testing the
entry was not working correctly. Upon examination it was clear
that `="")`, near the end of the line should be `=="");` as
it is in the last name test. The test was not set up as a
comparison but rather as an assignment.

?

Did you know?

**Understanding the difference between comparison
and assignment**

A difficult concept when learning JavaScript is the use of
the equals sign. One equals sign between values is an
assignment. For example `A=B` means set B to equal A.
When a set of two equals signs is used, it is to compare
the two values and have either a true or a false result. So if
A=10 and B=10 then `A==B` is true. By the way, to test if
two variables are not equal, use the `!=` operator.

Working with text

Introduction

Learning how to manipulate text provides a bevy of methods to apply to your web pages. You can have JavaScript return a simple count of characters, or do something as complex as scramble words and make an anagram.

On the technical side, JavaScript has a dedicated `String` object. Objects have properties and methods. For example, `length` is a property of a text string. It tells a fact about the text. A method does something to a text string. The `replace` method replaces some characters with others. The `concat` method joins text strings together into one. In this chapter you will learn how to use these properties and methods.

What you'll do

Find out how long a word or phrase is

Isolate a part of a text string – a substring

Trim leading and trailing spaces

Test if a text string is found within a larger text string

Replace text

Combine text

Break apart a text string into smaller strings

Typical text applications

Splitting text apart, changing text and performing other manipulations are often needed procedures. A most basic property – `length` – is useful to make sure a word or phrase is the correct number of characters. Phone numbers, postal codes, etc., all need to conform to a certain length.

Some key methods are:

- `concat` – join strings together
- `split` – break a string apart
- `replace` – swap a string of text for another string
- `substr` – extract a part of a string

Jargon buster

A **string** is synonymous with **text**. The words are interchangeable, but also can be referred to as a single entity – a text string.

There are a number of reasons for checking character count. The typical place to check the count is when submitting a web form. Character counting is an important part of validation, for example:

- checking that required fields do not have a character count of 0
- checking that certain types of data adhere to the expected length
- checking that an entered string of text does not exceed a perceived reasonable length.

The last bullet point above is useful in avoiding malicious behaviour. Some devious hackers or identity thief types may try to send a database query through a form's entry box, in an attempt to have the server return confidential information. Therefore allowing an arbitrary value of, say, 25 characters for a first name allows a validation check to reject any count above that. Most database queries have to be longer than that.

The `length` property returns the count of a text string. Figure 2-1 shows a simple form to demonstrate this.

Figure 2-1 A message from a script

In this example, a word or phrase is entered and the button is clicked. A popup message tells the count of characters. Listing 2-1 contains the HTML and JavaScript that make up this exciting demonstration.

Counting the characters in a text string (cont.)

Listing 2-1 Counting characters

```html
<html>
<head>
<title>Brilliant JavaScript</title>
<style>
body {font-family:arial,helvetica,sans-
serif;font-weight:bold;
    background-color:#aaddff}
</style>
<script type="text/javascript">
function countme() {
   t=document.getElementById("text1"). value;
    alert (t + " is " + t.length + "
    characters long");
}
</script>
</head>
<body>
<br /><br />
<form name="form1" onSubmit="countme()">
Enter a word or phrase<br />
<input type="text" id="text1" size="30" />
<br /><br />
<input type="submit" value="Click Me" />
</form>
</body>
</html>
```

The meat of the matter for this example is the `countme` function. In this function a variable, `t`, is set to the text entered in the box, and an alert is used to show the count, by using the `length` property:

```
t=document.getElementById("text1"). value;
alert (t + " is " + t.length + "
characters long");
```

Since this occurs in a function, some action has to call the function for the count to happen. The calling action occurs when the button is clicked. This submits the form; in the form tag the `onsubmit` event is what taps the function:

```
<form name="form1" onSubmit="countme()">
```

For your information

Something to consider

The `length` property counts letters, numbers, punctuation and spaces. Spaces can be a problem. If 10 spaces were typed into the form, the character count would be 10, even though nothing seems to be there. Many programming languages have a 'trim' function, which removes spaces from the beginning and/or end of a text string. JavaScript does not have a trim function. Instead a bit of ingenuity using the `substring` method will do. Coming up next …

Getting a part of a text string

There are two similar methods for pulling out a piece of a text string:

- `substr` – extracts a given number of characters from a given starting point
- `substring` – extracts characters between given start and stop positions.

Listing 2-2 shows these two methods in action. Here the output is written to the page after the button is clicked. The 'Click Me' button has the `extract()` JavaScript function as the target of its click event. Two portions of the phrase entered in the text box appear on the page. The first line 'A rose' is placed with the use of the `substr` method, and 'is a rose' is pulled from the phrase using the `substring` method.

These five lines are the contents of the `extract` function:

```
mytext=document.getElementById("text1").
value;
  var place1=document.getElementById
  ("place1");
  var place2=document.getElementById
  ("place2");
  place1.innerHTML=mytext.substr(0,6);
  place2.innerHTML=mytext.substring (17,40);
```

One by one, the lines do this:

1. Store the text from the text box in a variable named **mytext**.

2. Set the variable **place1** to represent a **div** section of the same name (see Chapter 7).

3. Set the variable **place2** to represent a div section of the same name

4. Set the **innerHTML** property of **place1** to 'A rose' by using the **substr** method to pull the first 6 characters

5. Set the **innerHTML** property of **place2** to 'is a rose' by using the **substring** method to pull all the characters from the 18th position to the end of the string

Listing 2-2 Isolating parts of a text string

```html
<html>
<head>
<title>Brilliant JavaScript</title>
<style>
body {font-family:arial,helvetica,sans-
serif;font-weight:bold;
      background-color:#bbddaa}
</style>
<script type="text/javascript">
function extract() {
  mytext=document.getElementById
  ("text1").value;
  var place1=document.getElementById
  ("place1");
  var place2=document.getElementById
  ("place2");
  place1.innerHTML=mytext.substr(0,6);
  place2.innerHTML=mytext.substring (17,40);
}
</script>
</head>
<body>
<br />
<form name="form1" >
Enter a word or phrase<br />
<input type="text" id="text1" value="A rose
is a rose is a rose" size="30" />
<br /><br />
<input type="button" value="Click Me"
onclick="extract()" />
</form>
<hr />
<div id="place1"></div>
<br />
<div id="place2"></div>
</body>
</html>
```

Getting a part of a text string (cont.)

Figure 2-2 shows the resulting web page.

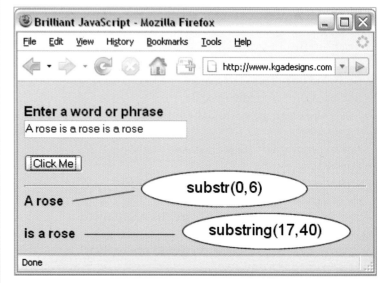

Figure 2-2 Placing text portions on the web page

Creating a custom trim method

Listing 2-3 includes a JavaScript function, **trim**, that strips away any spaces from the beginning and/or the end of the entered text. Two **while** loops are used. The first removes leading spaces and the second removes trailing spaces.

Listing 2-3 Getting a trim

```
<html>
<head>
<title>Brilliant JavaScript</title>
<style>
body {font-family:arial,helvetica,sans-
serif;font-weight:bold;
     background-color:#bbddaa}
</style>
<script type="text/javascript">
function trim(mytext) {
  mytext=document.getElementById
  ("text1").value;
  startlength=mytext.length
```

**Getting a part of
a text string
(cont.)**

```
    var result=document.getElementById
    ("result");
  // repeat as long as the first position is
a space
  while (mytext.substring(0,1) == ' ') {
    // the first character (a space) is
    removed
    mytext = mytext.substring(1,
    mytext.length);
  }
  // repeat as long as the last position is
  a space
  while (mytext.substring(mytext.length-1,
  mytext.length) == ' ') {
    // the last character (a space) is
removed
    mytext = mytext.substring(0,mytext.length-
1);
  }
result.innerHTML=mytext + " had " +
startlength + " characters and now has " +
mytext.length;
}
</script>
</head>
<body>
<br />
<form name="form1" >
Enter a word or phrase<br />
<input type="text" id="text1" size="30" />
<br /><br />
<input type="button" value="Click Me"
onclick="trim()" />
</form>
<hr />
<div id="result"></div>
</body>
</html>
```

2

Getting a part of a text string (cont.)

Figure 2-3 shows how the entered text has leading spaces (trailing ones too, but you can't see them). The button has already been clicked, running the function – which reports the before and after character counts.

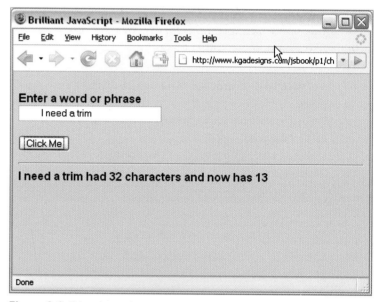

Figure 2-3 Trimming out spaces

In some applications it is necessary to see if one text string is inside another. Additionally, if a smaller string is found inside a larger one, where inside the larger string does it start?

Inventory and accounting systems, for example, are known for using strings of alphanumeric characters as containers of important data. For example, MMW672D22R may contain a part identification number within the string.

Listing 2-4 contains a JavaScript routine that tests for two part numbers, D24 and D22, within the larger string. The **indexOf** method is used here. If the smaller string is in the larger one, **indexOf** will return its starting position (based on zero indexing). If the string is not found the method returns –1. In the script, **if** statements test for the part numbers and the appropriate results are written to the page.

Listing 2-4 Searching for one string inside another

```
<html>
<head>
<title>Brilliant JavaScript</title>
<style>
body {font-family:arial,helvetica,sans-
serif;font-weight:bold;
    background-color:#eeffee}
</style>
<script type="text/javascript">
 var biglongstring="MMW672D22R";
 startpos=biglongstring.indexOf("D24");
 if (startpos==-1) {
    document.write ("<br />Part D24 not
found");
 } else {
    document.write ("<br />Part D24 starts
at position " + (startpos + 1));
 }
 startpos=biglongstring.indexOf("D22");
 if (startpos==-1) {
    document.write ("<br />Part D22 not
found");
 } else {
```

Finding where a string starts inside a larger string (cont.)

```
    document.write ("<br />Part D22 starts
at position " + (startpos + 1));
  }
</script>
</head>
<body>
</body>
</html>
```

The large string is set to the appropriately named variable, **biglongstring**. The line after contains the test using **indexOf**, which is structured as a method of the larger string, with the string to search for in the parentheses:

```
var biglongstring="MMW672D22R";
startpos=biglongstring.indexOf("D24");
```

Figure 2-4 shows the output. Since the script is not a function, it runs when the page loads.

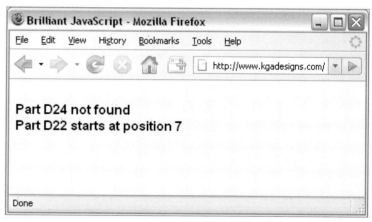

Figure 2-4 Searching for strings in strings

The JavaScript string object includes a `replace` method. Replacing text is useful in many situations. One comes to mind immediately – changing personal information. A person is married and the last name needs to be changed. Someone moves and the address needs an update, and so on.

Listing 2-5 offers a simple example of the `replace` method. The routine replaces 'Jack and Jill went for a jog' with 'Walter and Wendy went for a walk'.

Listing 2-5 Replacing text

```html
<html>
<head>
<title>Brilliant JavaScript</title>
<style>
body {font-family:arial,helvetica,sans-
serif;font-weight:bold;
    background-color:#cceeee}
</style>
<script type="text/javascript">
 var output="";
 mytext="Jack and Jill went for a jog";
 output=output + mytext + "<br /><br />";
 mytext=mytext.replace("Jack","Walter");
 mytext=mytext.replace("Jill","Wendy");
 mytext=mytext.replace("jog","walk");
 output=output + mytext + "<br /><br />";
 document.write (output);
</script>
</head>
<body>
</body>
</html>
```

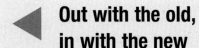

Out with the old, in with the new

2

Figure 2-5 shows the before and after text strings.

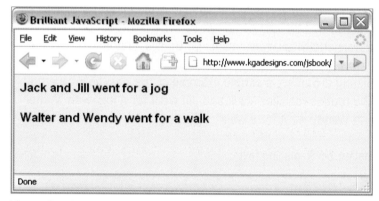

Figure 2-5 Text, replaced

The `replace` method is case sensitive. In the Listing 2-5 code, walk replaces jog, as in:

```
mytext=mytext.replace("jog","walk");
```

If perchance the line was coded with jog as Jog or JOG, the replacement would not occur. The case sensitivity can be overridden, though. To apply case insensitivity the string that is to be replaced is given a switch, **i**. In addition, the string is not put in quotes but instead is sandwiched between slashes:

```
mytext=mytext.replace(/JOG/i,"walk");
```

Since JOG is within slashes, and a lower case i follows the second slash, the replace will still work.

Any number of text strings can be combined into one longer string. There are two ways to go about this. One way is to concatenate them using the concatenate operator '+' – a plus sign for maths, but not for words! This short script demonstrates using the concatenation operator:

```
<script type="text/javascript">
   text1="Putting";
   text2="words";
   text3="together";
   document.write(text1 + " " + text2 + " "
   + text3)
</script>
```

The output of this script is 'Putting words together'.

An alternative approach is to use the **concat** method. A single use of **concat** allows multiple strings to be put together. Listing 2-6 contains a script that combines the individual strings by using the **concat** method. To point out the importance of considering that the space between two words is itself a string, the script displays two successive popups. The first is without spaces between the words, the second does have spaces.

Listing 2-6 Combining text strings

```
<html>
<head>
<title>Brilliant JavaScript</title>
<style>
body {font-family:arial,helvetica,sans-
serif;font-weight:bold;
      background-color:#cceeee}
</style>
<script type="text/javascript">
   text1="Putting";
   text2="words";
   text3="together";
alert (text1.concat(text2, text3));
alert (text1.concat(" ",text2," ", text3));
</script>
</head>
```

Combining text

2

Combining text (cont.)

```
<body>
</body>
</html>
```

The **concat** method is applied as a member of the first string, and then within the method the other strings are listed:

```
text1.concat(" ",text2," ", text3)
```

Figure 2-6 shows the two successive alert popups. Clearly the second is in better shape with regard to readability.

Figure 2-6 Variations of combining text strings

As seen above, text strings can be combined with the `concat` method. The opposite action is accomplished with the `split` method. The one caveat is that with `split` you have to select which character indicates where to break the string up.

Imagine a list of names, separated with commas but no spaces:

Zak,Yvette,Xavier,Woodrow,Vernon,Usher,Terry-Ann

Separating these is easy as the comma serves as the character on which to break apart the names into distinct strings. For a bit of excitement this example breaks the string apart and populates an array with the separated names. Check this out in Listing 2-7.

Listing 2-7 Populating an array with a split string

```
<html>
<head>
<title>Brilliant JavaScript</title>
<style>
body {font-family:arial,helvetica,sans-
serif;font-weight:bold;
    background-color:#ffff00}
</style>
<script type="text/javascript">
  var friends="Zak,Yvette,Xavier,
  Woodrow,Vernon,Usher,Terry-Ann";
  var friend_array = new Array;
  friend_array=friends.split(",");
  for ($i=0;$i<friend_array.length;$i++) {
    document.write (friend_array[$i] + "<br
    />");
  }
</script>
</head>
<body>
</body>
</html>
```

Breaking up is easy to do

2

Breaking up is easy to do (cont.)

The `friend_array` is handed the names of the friends, and then a `for` loop is used to display them, one per line:

```
friend_array=friends.split(",");
  for ($i=0;$i<friend_array.length;$i++) {
    document.write (friend_array[$i] + "<br
    />");
  }
```

The output is shown in Figure 2-7.

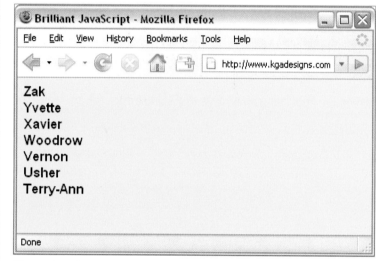

Figure 2-7 Splitting, storing and displaying a string

Jargon buster

The separator is also known as the **delimiter**. Common delimiters are commas, semicolons, spaces and tabs, although any character can be used, as long as it is used consistently throughout the larger string.

Working with numbers and mathematics

Introduction

Calculations abound within all applications, and web pages are part of the party. HTML has no ability to manipulate, calculate or summarise data. Yet think of all the calculators, polls, graphs and other numeric based interfaces there are on the net. Maths is going on somewhere in all this!

Actually maths is being performed in two places, on servers and in browsers. Browser-based calculations are managed with JavaScript. JavaScript has dedicated `Number` and `Math` objects. With these two powerhouses browsers can deliver a good amount of numeric ability.

Operating the operators

Multiplication, division, addition and subtraction have standard operators: `*`, `/`, `+`, `-`

Past these, further mathematical operators and operations can differ in various programming languages, so here is a summary of a how JavaScript manages a few popular numeric items:

`%` is the modulus operator (returns the fractional part of a division operation)

`++` increments a number

`--` decrements a number

`PI` returns the value of pi

`sqrt(x)` returns the square root of x

`pow(x,y)` returns x raised to the power of y

The four main maths operations are as standard in JavaScript as they are on the calculator sitting on your desk. No surprises here. That being said, Listing 3-1 shows a script that runs through the basic maths operations.

Listing 3-1 Basic maths operations

```
<html>
<head>
<title>Brilliant JavaScript</title>
<style>
body {font-family:arial;font-
weight:bold;background-color:#ffffcc}
</style>
<script type="text/javascript">
  x=5;
  y=10;
  z=20;
  document.write("x=" + x + " y=" + y + "
  z="  + z + "<br /><br /><br />");
  document.write("x + y + z = " + (x + y +
  z) + "<br /><br />");
  document.write("x * y * z = " + (x * y *
  z) + "<br /><br />");
  document.write("(x + y) * z = " + ((x +
  y) * z) + "<br /><br />");
  document.write("(z - x) * z = " + ((z -
  x) * z) + "<br /><br />");
  document.write("(x + y + z) / (x * x) = "
  +
     ((x + y + z) / (x * x)) + "<br /><br
     />");
  document.write("(y * y / z) / (x-z/x) + x
  = " +
     ((y * y / z) / (x-z/x) + x) + "<br
     /><br />");
</script>
</head>
<body>
</body>
</html>
```

3

If you wish, take a calculator and double-check the answers. Remember to follow the placement of parentheses!

Basic maths (cont.)

Figure 3-1 shows the output of the script in Listing 3-1.

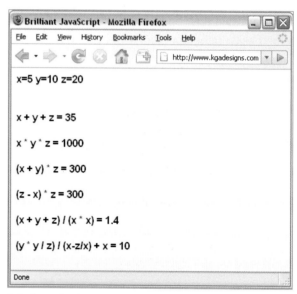

Figure 3-1 Some basic maths

This is an appropriate place for a quick maths refresher about how parentheses are used in formulas. Parentheses take precedence over the mathematical operators, meaning that calculations with parentheses are evaluated first. Some examples:

2 * 3 + 4 = 10

(2 * 3) + 4 = 10 (in this case the parentheses did not alter the order of the calculations)

2 * (3 + 4) = 14

5 + 6 / 8 + 9 = 14.75

(5 + 6) / 8 + 9 = 10.375

(5 + 6) / (8 + 9) = 0.647

Rounding it out

Rounding numbers is useful for presentation. For example, it is just as well to say 'I have 55 pounds in my pocket' than to say that you actually have '55 pounds and 10p'. That's a case of rounding down. Rounding can be performed in number of variations. Here are some examples:

- 55.10 rounded down equals 55
- 55.10 rounded up equals 56
- 55.10 truncated equals 55 (truncated here means dropping off the decimal portion of the number)
- 55.1839 rounded to three decimal positions equals 55.184
- 55.1839 rounded to two decimal positions equals 55.18

In terms of JavaScript the following functions are used for rounding: `floor`, `ceil`, `round` and `toFixed`.

Figure 3-2 shows how two values are handled with these functions.

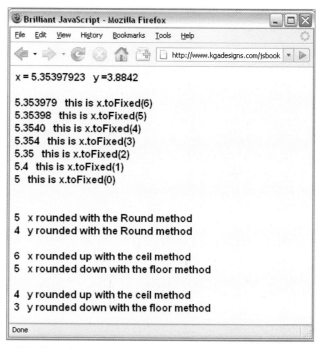

Figure 3-2 Rounding examples

The value of **x** in Figure 3-2 is purposely set to a number with the first decimal digit (3) being low, and the value of **y** is purposed set to a high first decimal digit (8). The `round` method simply rounds the number to the nearest integer, regardless of the number of decimal places. This is useful for quickly changing a number with multiple decimal digits to the closest integer. For a bit more control, the `ceil` method raises a decimal number up to the next higher integer, and the `floor` method lowers a decimal number to the next lower integer. The `ceil` and `floor` methods give you more control, because a number such as **x** can be rounded up to 6, and a number such as **y** can be rounded down to 3. If the `round` method was used, these numbers respectively would become 5 and 4, with no choice about it.

Listing 3-2 contains the script that created the output in Figure 3-2.

Listing 3-2 Applying rounding techniques

```
<script type="text/javascript">
  x=5.35397923;
  y=3.8842;
  document.write ("x = " + x +
"   y =" + y + "<br /><br
/>");
  document.write(x.toFixed(6) +
    "   this is
    x.toFixed(6)<br />");
  document.write(x.toFixed(5) +
    "   this is
    x.toFixed(5)<br />");
  document.write(x.toFixed(4) +
    "   this is
    x.toFixed(4)<br />");
  document.write(x.toFixed(3) +
    "   this is
    x.toFixed(3)<br />");
  document.write(x.toFixed(2) +
    "   this is
    x.toFixed(2)<br />");
  document.write(x.toFixed(1) +
```

Jargon buster

An **integer** is a number without any decimal or fractional part. 5 is an integer; 5.02 is not an integer. A **real number** is a number that can have a decimal part. 5.02 is a real number, but plain old 5 is also a real number. Think of it in terms of 5.00. Taken another way, 5 can be used in both integer and real number calculations. This actually has more to do with how databases store numbers, but this knowledge could be helpful in your JavaScript pursuits.

3

Rounding it out (cont.)

For your information

What the heck is   seen throughout Listing 3-2? That is the HTML code for a space, actually a 'non-breaking space' (therefore the acronym). In HTML any string of spaces is treated as a single space. For best formatting, successive HTML coded spaces can be used to create a string of multiple spaces, so   is a string of three spaces. I used these here for better presentation in the browser.

```
    "   this is
    x.toFixed(1)<br />");
document.write(x.toFixed(0) +
    "   this is
    x.toFixed(0)<br />");
document.write("<br /><br />");
document.write(Math.round(x) +
    "   x rounded with the
    Round method<br />");
document.write(Math.round(y) +
    "   y rounded with the
    Round method<br />");
document.write("<br />");
document.write(Math.ceil(x) +
    "   x rounded up with
    the ceil method<br />");
document.write(Math.floor(x) +
    "   x rounded down with
    the floor method<br />");
document.write("<br />");
document.write(Math.ceil(y) +
    "   y rounded up with
    the ceil method<br />");
document.write(Math.floor(y) +
    "   y rounded down with
    the floor method<br />");
</script>
```

The methods used here are:

- **toFixed(x)** – rounds a number up or down to the specified number of decimal places
- **Math.round(x)** – rounds to the closest integer
- **Math.ceil(x)** – rounds up to the next higher integer
- **Math.floor(x)** – rounds down to the next lower integer.

Who got the best grade? What is the least expensive price found for a litre of petrol? On which day did we have the most customers?

Questions like these are asked all the time. Essentially it's a question of what is the highest number, or what is the lowest number? The JavaScript `Math` object has two methods – `min` and `max` – that compare two values and return the appropriate minimum or maximum number. The syntax is structured like this:

`Math.min(x, y)` and `Math.max(x, y)`. These methods are useful only when evaluating variables that have changing values. This is obvious if you can consider that you can create a line such as

```
document.write(Math.min(4,5));
```

In this case you already know that 4 is smaller than 5!

Listing 3-3 contains a routine that uses `min` and `max`, but also shows a way to evaluate any number of values to find the minimum and maximum values.

Listing 3-3 Finding the low and high values

```
<html>
<head>
<title>Brilliant JavaScript</title>
<style>
body {font-family:arial;font-
weight:bold;background-color:#ffffcc}
</style>
<script type="text/javascript">
  x=4;
  y=6;
  document.write(Math.min(x,y) + "<br />");
  document.write(Math.max(x,y) + "<br />");
  // here is how to look for low and high
  values
  // among multiple numbers
  var nums=new Array(12, 7, 1, 8, 22, 10);
  highnum=nums[0];
  lownum=nums[0];
```

```
for ($i=0;$i<nums.length;$i++) {
    if (nums[$i]>highnum) {
        highnum=nums[$i];
    }
    if (nums[$i]<lownum) {
        lownum=nums[$i];
    }
}
document.write("<br /><br />The highest
number is " + highnum);
document.write("<br /><br />The lowest
number is " + lownum);
</script>
</head>
<body>
</body>
</html>
```

In Listing 3-3 an array is created and populated with multiple numbers. The initial low and high values are set to the first number in the array. Then a **for** loop goes through the array and tests if the current array's value is higher and lower. If/when these are true, the placeholder high and low values are overwritten. At the end of the loop the **highnum** and **lownum** variables contain the highest and lowest values. Neat!

```
var nums=new Array(12, 7, 1, 8, 22, 10);
    highnum=nums[0];
    lownum=nums[0];
    for ($i=0;$i<nums.length;$i++) {
        if (nums[$i]>highnum) {
            highnum=nums[$i];
        }
        if (nums[$i]<lownum) {
            lownum=nums[$i];
        }
    }
```

Figure 3-3 shows the output.

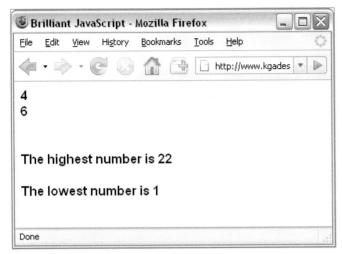

Figure 3-3 Finding high and low values

Getting powered up

A quick refresher. Raising a number to a given power is the equivalent of multiplying the number by itself over and over again to match the number indicated for the power. So, 2 to the fourth power (2^4), is the same as calculating 2 * 2 * 2 * 2. With either calculation, the answer is 16.

It becomes unwieldy to create a long equation of a number being multiplied by itself. Take 2 to the 12th power and you would need to enter 2 * 2 * 2 * 2 * 2 * 2 * 2 * 2 * 2 * 2 * 2 * 2 to get an answer.

The happy fix to this is to use the **pow** method of the **Math** object. Calculating 2 to the 12th power is then easily written as **Math.pow(2,12)**.

Listing 3-4 shows a few results returned using the **pow** method.

Listing 3-4 Powering up the numbers

```
<html>
<head>
<title>Brilliant JavaScript</title>
<style>
body {font-family:arial;font-
weight:bold;background-color:#eeffcc}
</style>
<script type="text/javascript">
document.write("2 raised to the twelfth
power equals " +
    Math.pow(2,12) + "<br />");
document.write("5 raised to the ninth power
equals " +
    Math.pow(5,9) + "<br />");
document.write("1 raised to the 1000th power
equals " +
    Math.pow(1,1000) + "<br />");
</script>
</head>
<body>
</body>
</html>
```

Figure 3-4 shows the result of using `pow`. The last calculation is there as food for thought; the number 1 multiplied by itself any number of times will always equal 1.

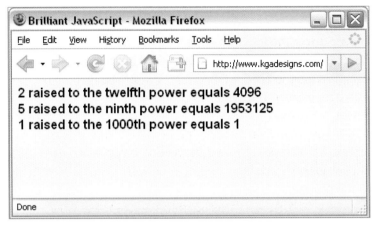

Figure 3-4 Raising numbers to powers

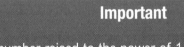

Important

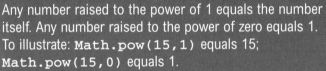

Any number raised to the power of 1 equals the number itself. Any number raised to the power of zero equals 1. To illustrate: `Math.pow(15,1)` equals 15; `Math.pow(15,0)` equals 1.

3

Random number generation

The ability to generate random numbers provides useful fodder for 'what-if' scenarios. Some applications are created to gauge risk about some future event; some game applications need random number generation to resemble the roll of dice, a spin of a wheel, etc.

The **random** method of the Math object provides a random number between 0 and 1. The generated number is several decimals long to ensure randomness when the method is called repeatedly. The syntax is simple, just `Math.random()`.

Listing 3-5 shows the **random** method being called five times in succession. Each time a number between 0 and 1 is written to the browser.

Listing 3-5 Generating random numbers

```html
<html>
<head>
<title>Brilliant JavaScript</title>
<style>
body {font-family:arial;font-
weight:bold;background-color:#eeeeff}
</style>
<script type="text/javascript">
document.write(Math.random() + "<br />");
document.write(Math.random() + "<br />");
document.write(Math.random() + "<br />");
document.write(Math.random() + "<br />");
document.write(Math.random() + "<br />");
</script>
</head>
<body>
</body>
</html>
```

Figure 3-5 shows how this appears. Bear in mind that every time this page is opened or refreshed a different set of numbers will appear.

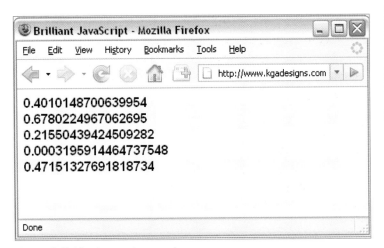

Figure 3-5 Viewing random numbers

The fact that **random** returns a decimal-based number between 0 and 1 is in itself not too useful. Applying a bit of maths to the number creates useful random numbers. For example, if you need random ages between 20 and 70, the random number needs to be not less than 20 and not more than 70, and since these are ages, the numbers should be integers. Here is a formula that will do just that:

```
document.write(Math.round(Math.random()*(70-
20) + 20)
```

In a nutshell, the **random** method is multiplied by a range that has a floor of the lowest needed value (20 in this case). Then the result is truncated into an integer using the **round** method.

Random number generation (cont.)

3

Calculating dates and times

Introduction

Using date and time calculations allows you to do nifty things such as count down the days to an event, see how many days have passed since you got your last oil change, or find out what day of the week your birthday will fall on. The `Date` object provides the methods to work with both dates and time. In this chapter you will find how to work with dates or time, independently of each other. A few methods learned in previous chapters, such as the rounding methods, help when calculating time-centric answers.

What you'll do

Return the current date and time

Work with the day, month and year components of the `Date` object

Work with the hour, minute and second components of the `Date` object

Use milliseconds to count time

Calculate the number of days in a range of dates

For your information

1 January 1970 is known as the epoch. This moment in time serves as a base for calculating date and time problems. To be clear, this is the day that Unix/Linux/Mac OS X/Java-based systems started the count. And the count marches on.

What day and time is it?

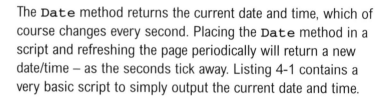

The `Date` method returns the current date and time, which of course changes every second. Placing the `Date` method in a script and refreshing the page periodically will return a new date/time – as the seconds tick away. Listing 4-1 contains a very basic script to simply output the current date and time.

Listing 4-1 The current date and time

```
<html>
<head>
<title>Brilliant JavaScript</title>
<style>
body {font-family:arial;font-
weight:bold;background-color:#eeeeff}
</style>
<script type="text/javascript">
var d = new Date();
document.write(d + "<br />");
</script>
</head>
<body>
</body>
</html>
```

First, a variable, `d` in this example, is set to an instance of the `Date` object. Then the value of the variable is written to the browser. Figure 4-1 shows the output. The full date and time are shown, perhaps a bit more information than is needed. The GMT –0400 value tells that I am 4 hours behind Greenwich Mean Time. GMT serves as a time base that other times and time zones are compared against.

Looking at the output in Figure 4-1 it is obvious that I made the screen shot at the 23rd minute of the 23rd hour of the day (ignoring the 35-second marker) – close to midnight.

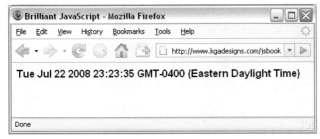

Figure 4-1 The current date and time

Jargon buster

`Date()` might be called a method but it's treated like an object. It is a method because it does something – it gets the current date and time. But it is instantiated like an object, and methods are used with it. Looks like an object, acts like an object. Must be an object.

Working with the month, day and year

Meaningful, readable output is made possible by isolating parts of the current date. A handful of methods provide the means to get the date parts that you need:

- `getDate` returns the numeric day value (1–31)
- `getMonth` returns the month value (0–11)
- `getFullYear` returns the four digit year value
- `getDay` returns the day of the week (0–6 with 0 being Sunday).

Figure 4-2 shows a more readable output of the date compared to Figure 4-1.

Figure 4-2 Date information

As succinct the message about the day and date appears in Figure 4-2, the script has some complexity to assemble such a message. Listing 4-2 shows the script code.

Listing 4-2 Returning a friendly representation of the date

```
<html>
<head>
<title>Brilliant JavaScript</title>
<style>
body {font-family:arial;font-weight:
bold;background-color:#eeeeff}
</style>
<script type="text/javscript">
var d = new Date();
var dd = d.getDate();
var days = new Array ("Sunday", "Monday",
```

```
"Tuesday", "Wednesday",
"Thursday", "Friday", "Saturday");
var months = new Array ("January",
"February", "March", "April", "May",
"June", "July", "August", "September",
"October", "November", "December");
message="Today is " + days[d.getDay()] + ",
";
ddstr=dd.toString();
switch (ddstr.substr(ddstr.length-1) {
    case "1":
      if ((ddstr.length==2) && (ddstr.
      substring(ddstr.length-2,1)==1)) ]
        message=message + "the " + dd + "th
        day of ";
      } else {
        message=message + "the " + dd + "st
        day of ";
      }
      break;
    case "2":
      if ((ddstr.length==2) &&
      (ddstr.substring(ddstr.length-
      2,1)==1)) {
        message=message + "the " + dd + "th
        day of ";
      } else {
        message=message + "the " + dd + "nd
        day of ";
      }
      break;
    default:
      message=message + "the " + dd + "th
      day of ";
}
message=message + month[d.getMonth()];
message=message " " + d.getFullYear();
document.write(message);
</script>
</head>
<body>
</body>
</html>
```

4

Working with the month, day and year (cont.)

See also

Arrays are explained in the next chapter.

In Listing 4-2 two arrays are created: **days** and **months**. These are used to take the numeric values from the **getDay** and **getMonth** methods respectively and return the equivalent string. For example, **getMonth** returns 6 for July and the sixth position in the **months** array is July. Embedding the **getMonth** method directly in as the index of the array makes for short and sweet coding:
months[d.getMonth()].

The switch construct is used to add the correct grammar for the specific day of the month. First, the numeric day of the month value is converted to a string. As a string the last character (a digit here) is tested to determine if it is 1, 2 or 3. The reasoning here is that any number ending in 1, 2 or 3 respectively is worded as, for example, the 21st, the 22nd or the 23rd. The suffixes for these numbers are 'st', 'nd' and 'rd'. The exception to this is the handling of the 11th, 12th and 13th of the month. These are handled in the if…then test. All other text equivalents of numeric dates get the 'th' suffix, for example the 18th or the 25th.

```
ddstr=dd.toString();
switch (ddstr.substr(ddstr.length-1)) {
   case "1":
      if ((ddstr.length ==2) && (ddstr.
      substring(ddstr.length-2,1)==1)) {
       message=message + "the " + dd + "th
       day of ";
      } else {
       messade=message + "the " + dd + "st
       day of ";
      }
      break;
```

Throughout the script in Listing 4-2, a user-friendly message is assembled, and that's what appears in Figure 4-2.

The time is always changing but at least with JavaScript you can capture it. With the `getHours`, `getMinutes` and `getSeconds` methods you can isolate those parts of the `Date` object. Remember that `Date` also contains a time component.

Using `Date` provides a high degree of precision – the returned value actually is in milliseconds. There are 86,400,000 milliseconds in a 24-hour period. JavaScript has a `getMilliseconds` method if you need to get down to such detail.

Listing 4-3 uses the appropriate methods to isolate the hour, minute and second. The values that come back from the methods are relative to the stroke of midnight. The values are put together into a message and written to the browser.

An additional method – `getTimezoneoffset` – returns, in minutes, how many time zones away the browser showing the result is from GMT (Greenwich Mean Time). This is also written to the browser. The result is first divided by 60 to transform it into hours.

Listing 4-3 Returning a friendly representation of the time

```
<html>
<head>
<title>Brilliant JavaScript</title>
<style>
body {font-family:arial;font-
weight:bold;background-color:#eeeeff}
</style>
<script type="text/javascript">
var d = new Date();
var m = d.getMinutes();
var h = d.getHours();
var s= d.getSeconds();
message="Since midnight  " + h + " hours, "
+ m +
        " minutes, and " + s + " seconds
        have passed";
document.write(message);
```

Important !

Calculating the offset from GMT can return an incorrect value. The calculation is based on the clock setting of the computer you are using. If the clock is not set to the correct time, then the calculation will be not return the correct offset to GMT. Further, treatment of Daylight Saving Time could alter the true offset.

4

```
message=" This is a " +
(d.getTimezoneOffset()/60) + " hour offset
from Greenwich Mean Time";
document.write("<br /><br />" + message);
</script>
</head>
<body>
</body>
</html>
```

Figure 4-3 shows the output.

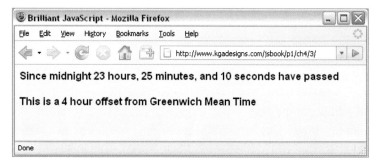

Figure 4-3 Time elapsed since midnight

Expanding on the ability to calculate time passing, here milliseconds are added to the mix. Figure 4-4 shows three messages that involve milliseconds:

 Getting granular with milliseconds

- the time passed since midnight, now including the milliseconds
- the time passed since midnight, reported just as milliseconds
- the time passed since the epoch (1 January 1970), in total milliseconds.

Figure 4-4 Reporting elapsed time in milliseconds

Some interesting mathematical equations were needed to transform the results to the millisecond level.

In the first line in Figure 4-4, the milliseconds value is simply the result of using the **getMilliseconds** method: **var ms=d.getMilliseconds();**

Converting the elapsed time since midnight into all milliseconds involves multiplying the hours, the minutes and the seconds by certain values.

- To convert seconds into milliseconds, multiply the seconds by 1000.
- To convert minutes into milliseconds, multiply the minutes by 60,000.
- To convert hours into milliseconds, multiply the hours by 3,600,000.

Getting granular with milliseconds (cont.)

In this example adding together the result of these calculations provides the total milliseconds since midnight, but only up to the second. The millisecond component is added too, and that sum is the number of milliseconds since midnight till 'this very moment':

```
var mstoday=((h * 3600000) + (m * 60000) +
(s *1000)) + ms;
```

To sum up the milliseconds since the epoch, the total milliseconds from midnight to 'this very moment' is added to the total milliseconds from the start of the epoch to the beginning of today: 12:00:00:00 am.

The total milliseconds of the day is already stored in the **mstoday** variable. The **UTC** method is used to get the milliseconds elapsed from the epoch to the beginning of today. **UTC** returns milliseconds from the epoch to the date entered into the **UTC** method. Putting 'today' in the **UTC** method provides the milliseconds from the epoch to the beginning of today. The **UTC** method needs the entered date to be in the form of (year, month, day), and the **getFullYear**, **getMonth** and **getDay** methods are used to get those values:

```
var totalms=Date.UTC(d.getFullYear(),
d.getMonth(), d.getDate());
```

Further in the script the **mstoday** and **totalms** values are added together for the full number of milliseconds till 'this very moment':

```
(totalms + mstoday)
```

Listing 4-4 contains the full script.

Listing 4-4 Boiling time down to milliseconds

```
<html>
<head>
<title>Brilliant JavaScript</title>
<style>
body {font-family:arial;font-
weight:bold;background-color:#eeeeff}
```

```
</style>
<script type="text/javascript">
var d = new Date();
var m = d.getMinutes();
var h = d.getHours();
var s= d.getSeconds();
var ms=d.getMilliseconds();
var mstoday=((h * 3600000) + (m * 60000) +
(s *1000)) + ms;
var totalms=Date.UTC(d.getFullYear(),
d.getMonth(), d.getDate());

message="Since midnight  " + h + " hours, "
+ m +
        " minutes, " + s + " seconds, and
        " + ms +
        " milliseconds have passed";
document.write(message);
message="Since midnight  " + mstoday
        + " milliseconds have passed";
document.write("<br /><br />" + message);
document.write("<br /><br />Since the epoch
" +
        (totalms + mstoday) + "
        milliseconds have passed");
</script>
</head>
<body>
</body>
</html>
```

Counting elapsed days

Much time-based maths is done at the millisecond level and counting days is no exception. This example calculates how many days have passed from a given date until 'today'. In this script the beginning date is hard-coded. The difference between the dates – literally the ending date (today) minus the beginning date – returns an answer in milliseconds. That answer is then divided by 86,400,000 (the number of milliseconds in one day) to convert the answer to days.

In Listing 4-5 the fixed date of 18 June 18 2008 is hard-coded as the beginning date.

Listing 4-5 Calculating the number of days between two dates

```
<html>
<head>
<title>Brilliant JavaScript</title>
<style>
body {font-family:arial;font-
weight:bold;background-color:#eeeeff}
</style>
<script type="text/javascript">
var date1= new Date("6/18/2008")
var date2 = new Date();
var months = new Array("January",
"February", "March", "April", "May",
                "June", "July",
                "August",
                "September",
                "October",
                "November",
                "December");


// 86400000 = 24 hours * 60 minutes * 60
seconds * 1000
// 86400000 is the number of milliseconds
in a day
diff=(date2 - date1) /86400000;
if (diff<2) {
    document.write (Math.floor(diff) +
    " day has passed since " +
    months[date1.getMonth()] +
    " " + date1.getDate());
```

```
  } else {
    document.write (Math.floor(diff) +
    " days have passed since " +
    months[date1.getMonth()] +
    " " + date1.getDate());
  }
</script>
</head>
<body>
</body>
</html>
```

Since the date difference calculation returns a decimal number, the `floor` method is used to present the answer in full days, instead of a day with a portion of it included. Figure 4-5 shows the result of the elapsed days calculation.

Figure 4-5 Counting how many days have passed

Calculating the number of days till a future date

Countdown calculations are often used with regard to important events, such as a birthday, a holiday, etc. In this example, the number of days between today and a future date is calculated. This is very similar to the previous example, just using the dates in the opposite order. Listing 4-6 shows the script used to calculate the number of days.

Listing 4-6 Calculating the number of days until a future event

```
<html>
<head>
<title>Brilliant JavaScript</title>
<style>
body {font-family:arial;font-
weight:bold;background-color:#eeeeff}
</style>
<script type="text/javascript">
var date1 = new Date();
var date2= new Date("10/12/2008")
var months = new Array("January",
"February", "March", "April", "May",
                              "June", "July",
"August", "September", "October",
                              "November",
"December");
if (date2 < date1) {
   document.write("The dates are not in the
correct order!");
} else {
// 86400000 = 24 hours * 60 minutes * 60
seconds * 1000
// 86400000 is the number of milliseconds
in a day
diff=(date2 - date1) /86400000;
document.write (Math.ceil(diff) +
    " day(s) until " +
months[date2.getMonth()] +
    " " + date2.getDate());
}
</script>
</head>
<body>
</body>
</html>
```

Figure 4-6 shows the output. In this example, the calculation is to return the number of days left from today until the hard coded date of 12 October 2008.

Figure 4-6   The number of days left

Getting organised with arrays

Introduction

Arrays are collections of like items. That is, an array is typically used to keep similar data together in an easily accessible construct, although there is no hard rule that the data elements have to have anything in common. The months of the year can be kept in an array. The names of your favourite rugby players can be kept in an array. A list of your customers can be kept in an array. The usefulness comes in when you need to use one, some or all of the elements of the array.

Jargon buster

The individual items of an array are called **elements**. Being of an elementary nature, an element is a singular piece of an array.

What you'll do

Learn how to create arrays

Manage individual array elements

Sort an array

Combine arrays

Creating an array

An array is an object and is therefore instantiated (which is a fancy way of saying you use a copy of the array object). An array is therefore declared with a name you decide, and set to be a 'new Array'. Pretty elementary. An example would be `var veggies = new Array;`

An array can be empty with no elements, but what's the point of that? Instead an array is populated with information. Each piece of information is an element. There is no limit to the number of elements. Listing 5-1 demonstrates creating two arrays: one for fruits and one for vegetables. These arrays are created the same way, using `new Array`, but are populated with different techniques. The `fruits` array is populated in the same line of code that creates the array. The `veggies` array is first created, and then populated one element at a time.

Listing 5-1 Creating arrays

```
<html>
<head>
<title>Brilliant JavaScript</title>
<style>
body {font-family:arial;font-
weight:bold;background-color:#eeeeff}
</style>
<script type="text/javascript">
var fruits = new Array("apples",
            "bananas", "cherries",
            "dragonfruit","elderberry",
            "fig", "gooseberry",
            "huckleberry");
var veggies = new Array;
veggies[0]="zucchini";
veggies[1]="yam";
veggies[2]="wild leek";
document.write("There are " + fruits.length
+ " fruits and " +
  veggies.length + " vegetables");
</script>
</head>
<body>
</body>
</html>
```

The **fruits** array is created and populated in one step. Including the array elements, separated by commas in a list – in the parentheses after the **Array** keyword – creates and populates the array:

```
var fruits = new Array("apples",
            "bananas", "cherries",
            "dragonfruit", "elderberry",
            "fig", "gooseberry",
            "huckleberry");
```

The script in Listing 5-1 creates the two arrays and simply reports how many elements each array has, by accessing the **length** property. Figure 5-1 shows the output.

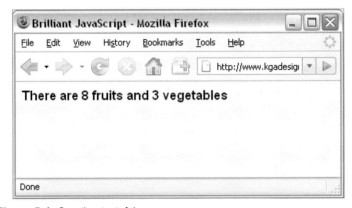

Figure 5-1 Creating tasteful arrays

For your information

Array elements are addressed using brackets. Therefore the first fruit, apples, can be accessed by using the syntax structure **fruits[0]**. As with many numerated JavaScript items, arrays are indexed zero-based. The first element is 0, and the last element is whatever the length property returns, minus 1.

5

Working with array elements

Arrays are great for storing data, but their real usefulness comes into play when you can work with individual elements. It is easy to use one element by simply supplying the index number, as in `veggies[2]`. This example shows how to focus on individual elements, add extra elements, remove elements, and reorder them as well. Let's get cracking!

Figure 5-2 reports various information about the `fruits` array. Each line tells something about the current state of the array.

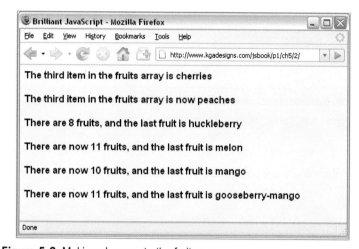

Figure 5-2 Making changes to the fruit array

Each line shown in Figure 5-2 tells of something that has changed in the array. Listing 5-2 contains the script that manipulates the array and writes out the lines to the browser.

Listing 5-2 Making fruitful array changes

```
<html>
<head>
<title>Brilliant JavaScript</title>
<style>
body {font-family:arial;font-
weight:bold;background-color:#eeeeff}
</style>
```

```
<script type="text/javascript">
var fruits = new Array("apples", "bananas",
            "cherries", "dragonfruit",
            "elderberry", "fig",
            "gooseberry", "huckleberry");
//return a single element
document.write("The third item in the fruits
array is " + fruits[2] + "<br /><br />");
//change the value of an element
fruits[2]="peaches";
document.write("The third item in the fruits
array is now " + fruits[2] + "<br /><br
/>");
// how many elements right now?
document.write("There are " + fruits.length
+ " fruits, and the last fruit is " +
fruits[fruits.length-1] + "<br /><br />");
//add new elements, a new fruit!
fruits.push("lemon","mango","melon");
document.write("There are now " +
fruits.length + " fruits, and the last
fruit is " + fruits[fruits.length-1] + "<br
/><br />");
fruits.pop();
document.write("There are now " +
fruits.length + " fruits, and the last
fruit is " + fruits[fruits.length-1] + "<br
/><br />");
fruits.push(fruits[6] + "-" + fruits[9]);
document.write("There are now " +
fruits.length + " fruits, and the last
fruit is " + fruits[fruits.length-1] + "<br
/><br />");
  </script>
</head>
<body>
</body>
</html>
```

5

Working with array elements (cont.)

The array is created with eight elements:

```
var fruits = new Array("apples", "bananas",
            "cherries", "dragonfruit",
            "elderberry", "fig",
            "gooseberry", "huckleberry");
```

The first output line lists the element count.

The next line reports back about a single element. By using the brackets and the index position, the individual fruit is selected for the output line:

```
document.write("The third item in the fruits
array is " + fruits[2]
```

With the zero-based indexing, the third element is represented by the number 2 (the element positions up to here being 0, 1, 2). Cherries is the third fruit.

An element is changed by simply assigning it a new value. Here, the third element is changed to peaches. The cherries were not tasty, but ah, the peaches are magnificent!

```
fruits[2]="peaches";
document.write("The third item in the fruits
array is now " + fruits[2]
```

At this point there are still eight elements in the array. The **push** method appends new elements to the end of the array. The **push** method contains any number of elements to be appended, three in this case:

```
fruits.push("lemon","mango","melon");
```

The **pop** method removes the last element:

```
fruits.pop();
```

The lines in the browser have now reported the new number of elements after using the **push** and **pop** methods.

Finally, a new element is created by combining two other elements. The **push** method puts this new element at the end of the array. The two elements that comprise the new element do not get altered. In other words they are not removed just because they are used somewhere else. The new element is independent from the two elements used to create it:

```
fruits.push(fruits[6] + "-" + fruits[9]);
document.write("There are now " +
fruits.length + " fruits, and the last
fruit is " + fruits[fruits.length-1] + "<br
/><br />");
```

5

Sorting an array

Array elements can be entered into the array in any order. When the elements need to be ordered, you can sort them to be in ascending or descending order. The sort and reverse methods are used here.

The script in Listing 5-3 creates an array of vegetables, sorts the array (**veggies.sort()**) and then reverses the order (**veggies.reverse()**).

Listing 5-3 Sorting an array

```
<html>
<head>
<title>Brilliant JavaScript</title>
<style>
body {font-family:arial;font-
weight:bold;background-color:#eeeeff}
</style>
<script type="text/javascript">
var veggies = new Array;
veggies[0]="zucchini";
veggies[1]="peas";
veggies[2]="corn";
veggies[3]="potatoes";
veggies[4]="asparagus";
veggies[5]="broccoli";
for (i=0;i<veggies.length;i++) {
   document.write("  " +
   veggies[i]);
}
document.write("<br /><br />");
veggies.sort();
for (i=0;i<veggies.length;i++) {
   document.write("  " +
   veggies[i]);
}
document.write("<br /><br />");
veggies.reverse();
for (i=0;i<veggies.length;i++) {
   document.write("  " +
veggies[i]);
}
</script>
```

```
</head>
<body>
</body>
</html>
```

Figure 5-3 displays the output of the array before the sort, after the sort, and after the sort is reversed.

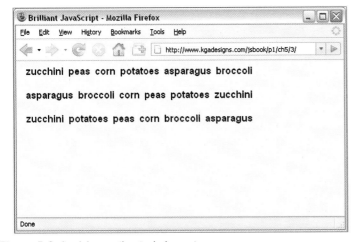

Figure 5-3 Applying sorting techniques to an array

Note that the **reverse** method reversed the sorted array, not the array as it was before the sort. Looking at the syntax, it could be misleading, since the **reverse** method is simply applied to the array. It is applied to the latest state of the array:

```
veggies.reverse();
```

Therefore the veggies array literally lost its original non-sorted order when the **sort** method was used. What if you need to revert the array back to its original state? A fallback approach works here in which the array is copied right after being created, creating essentially a backup of the array.

Backing up an array before sorting it

To do this, a second array is created and a **for** loop is used to copy the elements into the new array.

5

Sorting an array (cont.)

At the end of the script the original order is written by running through the second array. Listing 5-4 shows the updated script.

Listing 5-4 Saving a copy of an array before sorting it

```
<script type="text/javascript">
var veggies = new Array;
veggies[0]="zucchini";
veggies[1]="peas";
veggies[2]="corn";
veggies[3]="potatoes";
veggies[4]="asparagus";
veggies[5]="broccoli";
var veggies2 = new Array
for (i=0;i<veggies.length;i++) {
    veggies2[i]=veggies[i];
}
for (i=0;i<veggies.length;i++) {
   document.write("  " +
   veggies[i]);
}
document.write("<br /><br />");
veggies.sort();
for (i=0;i<veggies.length;i++) {
   document.write("  " +
   veggies[i]);
}
document.write("<br /><br />");
veggies.reverse();
for (i=0;i<veggies.length;i++) {
   document.write("  " +
   veggies[i]);
}
document.write("<br /><br />  The
original order is:<br />");
veggies.reverse();
for (i=0;i<veggies2.length;i++) {
   document.write("  " +
   veggies2[i]);
}
</script>
```

Figure 5-4 shows the output, in which the original order is written after the sort.

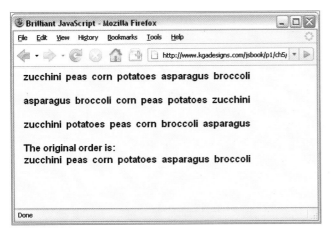

Figure 5-4 Writing the saved array copy

Sorting numbers

The `sort` method treats array elements as text. This is perfect for sorting words but does not work for sorting numbers. Although the `sort` method will sort numbers, they come out in a textual order. In other words, 30 comes before 4 because, as text, 3 comes before 4.

In Listing 5-5 an array, named `Lottery`, is created and populated with an unordered set of numbers. When the `sort` method is used, the sort is incorrect. This is seen later in Figure 5-5. The workaround is to have a function call embedded in the `sort` method, like this:

```
lottery.sort(bynumber);
```

The **bynumber** function doesn't have a returned value that is used by the array, but rather the action of just running a mathematical equation inside the function causes the sort to treat the values as true numbers. The function is simple:

```
function bynumber(a,b) {
  return a-b;
}
```

5

Sorting an array (cont.)

The parameters expected in the function declaration are not sent, yet the **a-b** calculation does the trick of letting the **sort** method know that the array values have to be treated as numbers.

Listing 5-5 Sorting an array of numbers

```html
<html>
<head>
<title>Brilliant JavaScript</title>
<style>
body {font-family:arial;font-
weight:bold;background-color:#eeeeff}
</style>
<script type="text/javascript">
var lottery = new Array(23,12,8,36,3,21);
for (i=0;i<lottery.length;i++) {
   document.write("  " +
   lottery[i]);
}
document.write("<br /><br />");
lottery.sort();
for (i=0;i<lottery.length;i++) {
   document.write("  " +
   lottery[i]);
}
document.write("<br /><br />");
lottery.sort(bynumber);
for (i=0;i<lottery.length;i++) {
   document.write("  " +
   lottery[i]);
}
function bynumber(a,b) {
 return a-b;
}
</script>
</head>
<body>
</body>
</html>
```

Figure 5-5 shows the array in its original order, followed by a standard sort, and then followed by the modified sort.

Figure 5-5 Sorting out the number-sorting issue

Combining arrays

Arrays can be assembled into larger arrays. The `concat` method appends one array to another. The method can append more than one array. The script in Listing 5-6 creates three arrays, and then runs the paces of combining them in different ways. At one point a new array is created as the result of concatenating two arrays.

Listing 5-6 Combining and concatenating arrays

```
<html>
<head>
<title>Brilliant JavaScript</title>
<style>
body {font-family:arial;font-
weight:bold;background-color:#eeeeff}
</style>
<script type="text/javascript">
var classroom_A = new
Array("Amy","Bob","Carolyn","Dave",
"Erin","Fred");
var classroom_B = new
Array("Grace","Harry","India","Jack",
"Karen");
var classroom_C = new
Array("Lenny","Mary","Nick","Opal","Pete");

document.write(classroom_A.concat
classroom_B));
document.write("<br /><br />");
document.write(classroom_A.concat
(classroom_B,classroom_C));
document.write("<br /><br />");
var classroom_D = new
Array(classroom_C.concat(classroom_A));
document.write(classroom_D);
</script>
</head>
<body>
</body>
</html>
```

Combining arrays (cont.)

Figure 5-6 shows the output from the script in Listing 5-6.

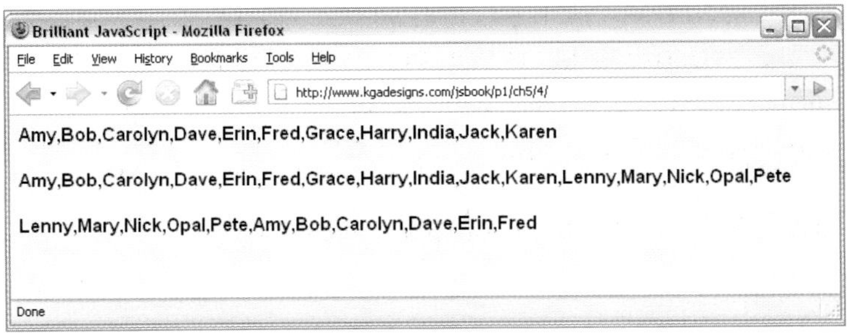

Figure 5-6 Combining arrays

Multidimensional arrays

Array elements can be arrays themselves, with their own elements. This structure is called a multidimensional array. There is no limit to how many arrays can be nested inside an array, but too many levels will be difficult to work with.

Demonstrated here is the creation of an array that contains elements and an array – which itself has an array inside it:

```
var continents = new
Array("Europe","Africa","Asia");
```

```
continents[0] = new
Array("France","Germany","Italy"
,"England");
continents[0][3] = new
Array("London", "Liverpool",
"Essex")
```

This structure is good for organisation, as here we have continents, countries and cities.
`continents[2]` returns Asia;
`continents[0][2]` returns Italy;
`continents[0][3][2]` returns Essex.

Validation

6

Introduction

Validation is absolutely one of the major uses of JavaScript. Coupled with online forms, validation run at the browser lets error-laden entries be caught and dealt with before any posting to the server. The advantage is in keeping the server free of unnecessary processing, which can cost performance. Validation at the browser level also reduces bandwidth use.

In this chapter a web-based form will be run through the validation marathon. Each section will add a type of validation.

Validate basic text entries

Validate numbers

Validate email addresses

Validate selections made with radio buttons and check boxes

Basic text entry validation

For your information

Functions return a single value. The 'type' of value can differ; it might be text, a number, or as in this case a boolean value. A boolean value is either true or false, or yes or no, or 1 or 0, or on or off, etc. The point is that there are only two logical values that a boolean value can be.

Figure 6-1 shows a simple web form. All that is required is your name and age.

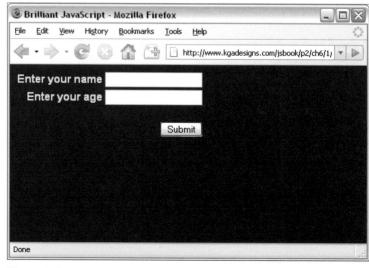

Figure 6-1 A simple web form

When the form is submitted via the Submit button, the validation function is called. The validation function (named `checkform`) has a number of successive tests (`if` statements). As soon as one fails, the function returns false. If all validation tests pass, the last line of the function, `return true`, is tapped, and because true is returned, the form can be submitted.

Listing 6-1 shows the code that makes up the form and the validation script.

Listing 6-1 A basic form and validation check

```
<html>
<head>
<title>Brilliant JavaScript</title>
<style>
td {font-weight:bold;text-align:right;}
body {background-
color:navy;color:yellow;font-family:Arial}
</style>
```

```
<script type="text/javascript">
function checkform() {
  if (document.getElementById
  ("txtName").value=="") {
    alert ("Must enter your name");
    return false;
 }
  if (document.getElementById("txtAge").
  value=="") {
    alert ("Must enter your age");
    return false;
  }
  if (isNaN(document.getElementById
  ("txtAge").value)) {
    alert ("Only numbers can be entered in
    the age box");
    return false;
  }
return true;
}
</script>
</head>
<body>
<form id="myform" action="" onsubmit="return
checkform()">
<table>
<tr><td>Enter your name</td><td><input
type="text" id="txtName" /></td></tr>
<tr><td>Enter your age</td><td><input
type="text" id="txtAge" /></td></tr>
<tr><td> </td><td><br /><input
type="submit" id="submit" value="Submit"
/></td></tr>
</table>
</form>
</body>
</html>
```

Examining the validation in detail, first the name is tested to be
present. This is done by using the **getElementById** method
to identify the text box, and then testing the length of the entry.
If it is an empty string (*""*) then an appropriate message
appears in an alert popup and the function returns false:

```
function checkform() {
  if (document.getElementById
  ("txtName").value=="") {
    alert ("Must enter your name");
    return false;
  }
```

Figure 6-2 shows what occurs when the form is submitted with no name.

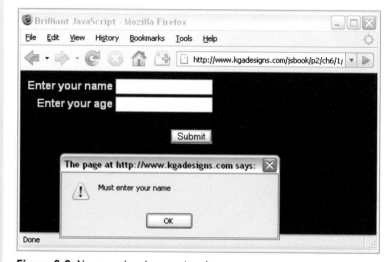

Figure 6-2 No name has been entered

When a name is entered, the test for the name passes and the routine moves down to the next test. Here an entered age is tested:

```
if (document.getElementById("txtAge").
value=="") {
  alert ("Must enter your age");
  return false;
}
```

Figure 6-3 shows what occurs when the form is submitted with no age.

Figure 6-3 No age has been entered

My age, 'ten', has been entered. Is this OK? No, because the next test is to see if the age entry is a number. This test is done with the **isNaN** (is not a number) function. Following the logic, literally, when it is true that the value is not a number, then false is returned:

```
if (isNaN(document.getElementById
("txtAge").value)) {
  alert ("Only numbers can be entered in
  the age box");
  return false;
}
```

Figure 6-4 shows the alert box that informs the user that only a real number can be entered for the age. Entering 'ten' does not trick the **isNaN** function into considering the entry to be 10.

Assuming that I have now entered a true number, such as 185, all tests pass and the value true is returned from the function. When this value is returned the form will submit and follows the action attribute (although none is indicated here in the form tag).

Basic text entry validation (cont.)

Figure 6-4 Only an actual number can go in the age box

Well, this is pretty good; I entered my name and an age of 185 and the validation did not catch any problems. However, there is a problem: I can't possibly be 185 years old. This type of realisation leads to the need for more validation. In particular, a test is added to make sure the age is between 1 and 100, like this:

```
the_age=document.getElementById("txtAge").val
ue;
if (the_age < 1 || the_age > 100) {
  alert ("The age must be between 1 and
  100");
  return false;
}
```

Figure 6-5 shows how I was caught pretending to be 185 years old.

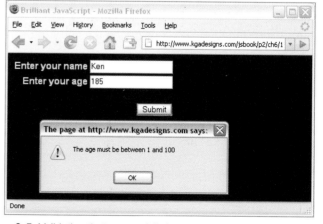

Figure 6-5 Validation that an age falls in an expected range

An email address has a few traits that make it identifiable as valid. These are having one and only one @ sign; having at least one dot; and if you want to get really serious, ensuring that the first and last characters are not the @ sign or a dot.

Email validation therefore is a small collection of mini-validations. Whereas you can probably code some long-winded single line of validation, using a handful of successive validations is easier to manage. This was the approach used in the previous section to validate age. Listing 6-2 contains the new JavaScript code to validate the email address.

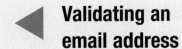

Listing 6-2 Validating an email address

```
if (document.getElementById("txtEmail").
value=="") {
    alert ("Must enter your email address");
    return false;
  }
  the_email=document.getElementById("txt
  Email").value;
  at_count=0;
  dot_count=0;
  for (i=0;i<the_email.length;i++) {
    if (the_email.substr(i,1)=="@") {
      at_count=at_count + 1;
    }
    if (the_email.substr(i,1)==".") {
      dot_count=dot_count + 1;
    }
  }
    if (at_count!=1) {
      alert ("There must be one @ sign in
      the email address");
      return false;
    }
    if (dot_count < 1) {
      alert ("There must be at least one
      dot (.) in the email address");
      return false;
    }
```

```
if (the_email.substr(0,1)=="@" ||
the_email.substr(the_email.length-
1,1)=="@" ||
    the_email.substr(0,1)=="." ||
    the_email.substr(the_email.length-
    1,1)=="."){
  alert ("The first and last characters
  cannot be @ or a dot(.)");
  return false;
}
```

The email validation:

■ checks that the length is greater than 0

■ loops through the email address and counts occurrences of the @ sign and the dot (.) – validation ensures there can be only one @ sign and at least one dot

■ examines the first and last characters to make sure they are neither an @ sign nor a dot.

Figure 6-6 shows an alert that either the @ sign is missing, or there are more than one of them.

Figure 6-6 Validating an email address

Radio buttons and check boxes are both boolean indicators. A button or check box is either checked or not. The difference between the two is that radio buttons are used for a mutually exclusive answer, which means that within a set of radio buttons, only one can be checked. If each radio button has the same name or id, then clicking one will clear the others. One caveat is that a form may open with no radio buttons checked. Validation can test this and send an alert to make a selection.

Check boxes are independent. Whether one is checked or cleared has no meaning to another check box. Where it could mean something is how the information needs to be handled from the human perspective. It might well be that only one check box should be checked because of a 'business rule'. Validation to the rescue!

Listing 6-3 is a section added to the validation function that tests the radio buttons and check boxes. On the form is now a question about driving and a question about tea. The driving question is answered using a radio button, and the tea question is answered with check boxes.

Listing 6-3 Validating radio buttons and check boxes

```
drivecheck = -1;
for (i=myform.drive.length-1; i > -1; i—) {
  if (myform.drive[i].checked) {
     drivecheck = i; i = -1;
  }
}
if (drivecheck == -1) {
  alert("Must select that you do or do not
  drive");
return false;
}
if (myform.teaplain.checked &&
myform.teamilk.checked) {
  alert ("Cannot check both plain tea and
  tea with milk");
  return false;
}
```

Validating radio buttons and check boxes (cont.)

Figure 6-7 shows the form with the new driving and tea questions. The validation tests that one of the radio buttons is checked – when the form opens both radio buttons are not checked. The validation also makes sure you cannot answer that you drink tea plain, and also drink it with milk. These two options are not possible together, at least not at the same time. In Figure 6-7 the message for the tea selection is displayed.

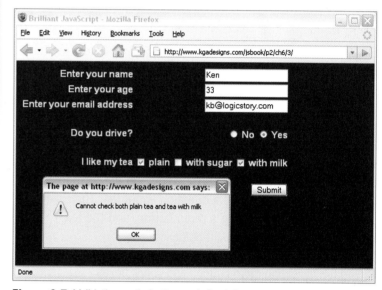

Figure 6-7 Validating radio button and check box selections

JavaScript has no dedicated method for date validation. There are many workarounds. Some use manipulations of the `Date` object, some use Regular Expressions (a pattern matching language), and others are just long code routines that attempt to take in every variation of date components.

A reasonable approach is to let users select the month, date and year from dropdowns. In this fashion the date is controllable, and with the ability to update one dropdown's list based on the selection in another dropdown, date validation becomes much easier because the person is not able to select an incorrect value. This is discussed in Chapter 7.

Further validation issues

Validation can be as long and complex as your needs are. Some validation needs that were not discussed in this chapter are:

■ Ensuring the correct length, such as with a phone number.

■ Validating numbers with regard to acceptable values. This was demonstrated with the age validation; however, there could be more complex needs such as allowing ages only between 10 and 20, and between 40 and 50.

■ Validation based on business rules. That was covered lightly in this chapter but there could be many rules that need to be accounted for. For example, anyone working in the Kensington office cannot be assigned to the marketing department; or if you selected that you do not drive, then you must select one of the methods of public transportation.

Applying JavaScript actions

7

Introduction

As with most modern languages, JavaScript is event-driven. This means that instead of an application following a fixed set of instructions or steps, the application is instead driven by the decisions a user makes. This has been the case for so long that it is not even pondered upon. But think about it for a moment. Unless specifically altered not to do this, a web page sits and waits for you to do something – click here, navigate there, select something from a list. All the 'actions' are taken as the person in front of the screen sees fit. Each action taken triggers an event.

An event is really just a shell within which you, as the programmer, decide what should happen. To bring this to a pointed example: there is a dropdown list on the web page. You decide to select an item from it. This action triggers the `onchange` event. However, there may or may not be any functionality that occurs. The event can get triggered, but if no coding is attached to the event then nothing happens.

There are many types of events, and each can occur upon certain actions for which the event makes sense. For example, there is an `onclick` event. This event can be used when there is something to click on (and assuming that the item being clicked on can recognise it is being clicked upon). The *de facto* click event is the one attached to a button on the page. More than anything else, a button's main purpose is to be clicked on.

What you'll do

Learn about events and how to trigger them

Use the `onchange` event to update and change web pages

Create an autosuggest feature

Use the `onfocus` and `onblur` events to provide easy visual aid

Jargon buster

An **event** might be referred to as, for example, the `onclick` event, or just the click event. The terms are interchangeable.

Events are always happening

Many events occur with a natural and expected behaviour that the browser takes care of. One of these is the load event. Every time a new page appears in a browser, or if the existing page is refreshed, the load event of the page runs. This does not mean that anything other than the page loading into the browser will occur; however, the load event can be used to perform other activities if there is a reason to do so. Events are called – that is, they are noted in the HTML by their name, and call a JavaScript routine or function. For example, the load event is called in the HTML body tag, like this:

```
<body onload="my_custom_action()">
```

Given this coding structure, presumably there is a JavaScript function named my_custom_action. What occurs in the function depends on what functionality you code into the event.

Another event is in constant play, not that you would necessarily notice it: onmousemove. A mouse is moved repeatedly while you are working at a computer. But if no custom program is placed in the event, then the event goes unnoticed.

Here is a summary of events. Each event applies to one or more objects, following a sense of logic. Clearly any event based on the mouse can only be used with mouse activities. In contrast the onchange event can be used when the selection in a dropdown list is changed, and also when text in a text entry box changes.

Events

onabort: triggered when an image load is interrupted

onblur: triggered when an element loses focus (e.g. tabbing out of a text box)

onchange: triggered when a dropdown selection or text is changed

onclick: triggered when certain objects are clicked (buttons, radio buttons, check boxes, etc.)

ondblclick: triggered when an object is double-clicked

onkeydown: triggered when a key is pressed

onkeypress: triggered when a key is pressed or held down

onkeyup: triggered when a key is let go

onload: triggered when the page or an image is finished loading

onmousedown: triggered when the mouse button is pressed

onmouseup: triggered when the mouse button is released

onmousemove: triggered as the mouse is moved

onmouseover: triggered when the mouse pointer is over a certain screen object

onmouseout: triggered when the mouse pointer is moved off a certain screen object

onreset: triggered when the special Reset button is clicked

onresize: triggered when the browser window is resized

Events are always happening (cont.)

onselect: triggered when text is selected

onsubmit: triggered when the submit button is clicked

onunload: triggered when the page is unloaded (such as when a page is exited)

Updating one select list based upon the selection in a different select list

Chapter 6 discussed how date validation is best controlled with dropdowns. This example shows that having dates selected from dropdown lists guarantees to provide valid dates. Listing 7-1 shows a script that runs when a selection is made in a dropdown list. When the page loads, the **months** select (dropdown) is populated with the names of the months, although the top item seen in the dropdown is a textual reminder of 'select a month'.

The second dropdown is for the days of the month, and it is this dropdown that starts out empty but gets populated with the correct number of days, as per the selected month, each time a different month is selected. Figure 7-1 shows the initial state of the form – with an empty **dates** dropdown.

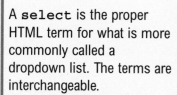
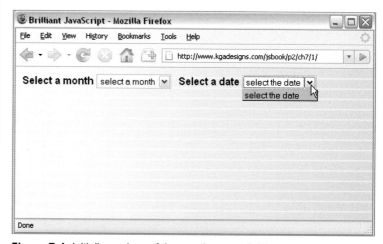

Figure 7-1 Initially no days of the month are available

In Figure 7-1 it is clear that the **dates** dropdown has no dates. This is because the page was just loaded and no month has been selected yet. Figure 7-2 shows the difference after a month is selected. The **dates** dropdown is filled with dates.

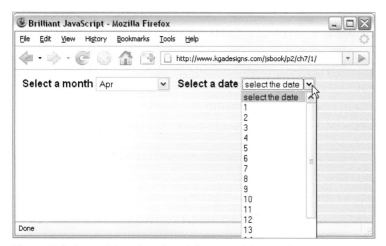

Figure 7-2 A month is selected, and the days of the month appear

Updating one
select list based
upon the selection
in a different
select list (cont.)

7

The `months` dropdown uses the `onchange` event to update the `dates` dropdown. That is, the change in one dropdown is used to update the contents of another one. Very handy! The `updatedays` function uses the value of the `months` dropdown to determine how many days are in the selected month, here in Listing 7-1.

Listing 7-1 Populating the days of the month, based on the selection of the month

```
<html>
<head>
<title>Brilliant JavaScript</title>
<style>
td {font-weight:bold;text-align:right;}
body {background-
image:url('smoothback1.jpg');color:black;fon
t-family:Arial}
</style>
<script type="text/javascript">
function updatedays() {
    dd=document.getElementById("dates");
    dd.options.length=0;
    dd.options[0]= new Option("select the
    date", 0)
    switch (document.getElementById
    ("months").value) {
```

```
      case "Jan":
      case "Mar":
      case "May":
      case "Jul":
      case "Aug":
      case "Oct":
      case "Dec":
         for (i=1;i<=31;i++) {
            dd.options[i] = new Option(i,i);
         }
         break;
      case "Apr":
      case "Jun":
      case "Sep":
      case "Nov":
         for (i=1;i<=30;i++) {
            dd.options[i] = new Option(i,i);
         }
         break;
      default:
         for (i=1;i<=28;i++) {
            dd.options[i] = new Option(i,i);
         }
         d = new Date();
         y = d.getFullYear();
         if (y==2008 || y==2012) {
            dd.options[29] = new
            Option(29,29);
         }
      }
   }
}
</script>
</head>
<body>
<form id="myform" action="#">
<table>
<tr><td>Select a month</td><td>
<select id="months" onchange="
updatedays()">
   <option value="none">select a
   month</option>
   <option value="Jan">Jan</option>
```

```
      <option value="Feb">Feb</option>
      <option value="Mar">Mar</option>
      <option value="Apr">Apr</option>
      <option value="May">May</option>
      <option value="Jun">Jun</option>
      <option value="Jul">Jul</option>
      <option value="Aug">Aug</option>
      <option value="Sep">Sep</option>
      <option value="Oct">Oct</option>
      <option value="Nov">Nov</option>
      <option value="Dec">Dec</option>
</select>
</td>
<td> </td>
<td>Select a date</td><td>
<select id="dates">
<option value="none">select the
date</option>
</select>
</td></tr>
</table>
</form>
</body>
</html>
```

The **months** select dropdown has the **onchange** event that calls the function:

```
<select id="months" onchange="updatedays
()">
```

The function first clears the **dates** dropdown, and sets the first option of 'select the date':

```
function updatedays() {
    dd=document.getElementById("dates");
    dd.options.length=0;
    dd.options[0]= new Option("select the
    date", 0)
```

Updating one select list based upon the selection in a different select list (cont.)

7

Important

Whenever there is a script that repopulates a **select** list, the list must first be cleared. If not, then the current list items will stay, and the new ones will be appended to the end. This is not what should be presented back on the page.

Updating one select list based upon the selection in a different select list (cont.)

A `switch` statement is used to determine how many days are in the month. Since all the months except February have a fixed number of days, the `switch` statement is set up such that multiple months are combined to receive the same number of days. For instance, when April, June, September or November is selected, the `dates` dropdown gets 30 days:

```
case "Apr":
    case "Jun":
    case "Sep":
    case "Nov":
        for (i=1;i<=30;i++) {
        dd.options[i] = new Option(i,i);
        }
```

The 30 days are populated using a loop that runs through 30 iterations. The other months have a loop of 31 iterations, except for February. February is handled a bit differently because of leap years. A loop of 28 iterations is run. Then a test for it being a leap year determines whether one more item (day 29) is appended. Note too that February is handled within the `default` section of the `switch`. This is feasible since the other 11 months are accounted for. February is the only possible month to hit the default.

```
default:
    for (i=1;i<=28;i++) {
        dd.options[i] = new Option(i,i);
    }
    d = new Date();
    y = d.getFullYear();
    if (y==2008 || y==2012) {
        dd.options[29] = new Option(29,29);
    }
}
```

Most navigation from one web page to another occurs from clicking a hyperlink. An alternative is to navigate to a web page or another website by selecting one from a dropdown list. Listing 7-2 shows a script that uses the item selected in a dropdown to be the page to navigate to. This clearly is possible when the values of the items in the dropdown are the actual web addresses (URLs).

Listing 7-2 Using a dropdown selection for web navigating

```html
<html>
<head>
<title>Brilliant JavaScript</title>
<style>
body {background-
image:url('back1.jpg');color:black;font-
family:Arial;font-weight:bold;}
</style>
<script type="text/javascript">
function go_somewhere() {
    var URL = document.getElementById
    ("sitelist").value;
    window.location.href = URL;
}
</script>
</head>
<body>
<form id="myform" action="#">
  Select a web site to visit:
  
<select id="sitelist" size=1
onchange="go_somewhere()">
<option value="">Go to....
<option
value="http://www.kgadesigns.com">KGA
Designs
<option
value="http://www.shakespearesplayground.com
">Shakespeare's Playground
<option
value="http://www.healingheartsandsouls.com"
>Healing Hearts and Souls
<option
value="http://www.logicstory.com">Logic
```

Navigating to another website from making a list selection

7

For your information

This example demonstrates the **onchange** event.

```
Story
</select>
</form>
</body>
</html>
```

When a selection is made in the dropdown, the **onchange** event calls the **go_somewhere** function:

```
function go_somewhere() {
    var URL = document.getElementById
    ("sitelist").value;
    window.location.href = URL;
}
```

The URL is taken from the value of the selected dropdown item, and the **window.location.href** construct is used to point the browser to the new site. When navigating there is a choice of having the new page load into the window that the current page is displayed in, or having the new page open in a new window.

A slight change of code tells the function to display the new page in a new window. In the case, the function would now be coded like this:

```
function go_somewhere() {
var URL = document.getElementById
("sitelist").value;
window.open (URL);
}
```

The single difference is that instead of using **window. location.href** to navigate, **window.open (URL)** is used. This instruction says simply to open a window and load the URL. Figure 7-3 shows how two windows are open: the window with the page with the dropdown, and the new window displaying the selected URL.

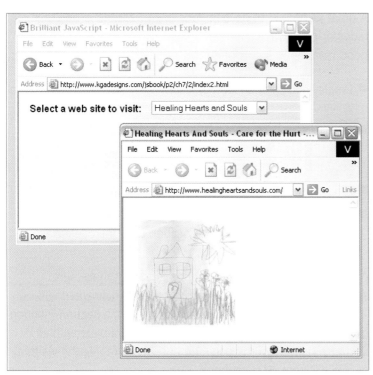

Figure 7-3 Using a new window to display a selected URL

Showing or hiding part of a page

A great technique to have in your box of scripts is one that hides or displays sections of a web page. There are plenty of good reasons to incorporate this functionality into a web page:

- Display a second section of a form only after the first section is filled in

- Display a particular section of a page depending on selections made in an initially visible section (the secondary sections are hidden until the selections are made)

- Hide or display sections depending on who is logged in

- If the page is presenting a test question or other Q and A content, display the 'answer' section after the question is completed

A standard way to display sections is to first make sure sections are built into the HTML. These are delineated with `<div></div>` tags; that is, a `div` defines a section (section being a loose term here). Figure 7-4 shows a page with all sections visible. On the page are buttons to toggle the visibility of two different `div` sections.

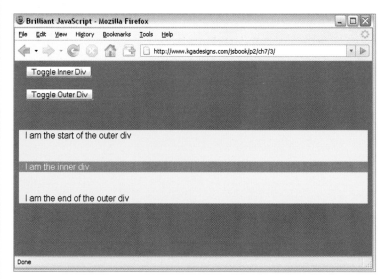

Figure 7-4 A page with `div` sections

To make this interesting, the `div`s are nested. There is an inner `div`, which is a part of the outer `div`. Using the buttons in varying sequence it is possible to display any combination of visibility. Both `div`s can be visible, the outer can be visible while the inner is not, the inner can be visible while the outer is not, or both can be hidden. Listing 7-3 shows the code.

Listing 7-3 A page with HTML `div`s and JavaScript to control their visibility

```
<html>
<head>
<title>Brilliant JavaScript</title>
<style>
td {font-weight:bold;text-align:right;}
body {background-
color:fuchsia;color:black;font-family:Arial}
</style>
<script type="text/javascript">
function toggle_innerdiv(){
var
innerdiv=document.getElementById("innerdiv")
;
if (innerdiv.style.visibility=="visible") {
    innerdiv.style.visibility="hidden";
  } else {
    innerdiv.style.visibility="visible";
}
}
function toggle_outerdiv(){
var outerdiv=document.getElementById
("outerdiv");
if (outerdiv.style.visibility=="visible") {
    outerdiv.style.visibility="hidden";
  } else {
    outerdiv.style.visibility="visible";
}
}
</script>
</head>
<body>
<form id="myform" action="#">
   <input type="button"
```

```
id="inner" value="Toggle Inner Div"
onclick="toggle_innerdiv()" />
<br /><br />
   <input type="button"
id="outer" value="Toggle Outer Div"
onclick="toggle_outerdiv()" />
</form>
<br /><br />
<div id="outerdiv" style="background-
color:yellow;">
   I am the start of the
outer div
<br /><br /><br />
<div id="innerdiv" style="background-
color:gray;color:white">
   I am the inner div
</div>
<br /><br />
   I am the end of the outer
div
</div>
</body>
</html>
```

Each button has an **onclick** event that calls one of two functions. Here is the one for the inner **div**:

```
<input type="button" id="inner"
value="Toggle Inner Div"
onclick="toggle_innerdiv()" />
```

The function tests the current visibility of the **div**. The possibilities are **visible** or **hidden**; and these two states belong to the **visibility** property. Whichever state is current gets replaced with the other – the visibility is toggled:

```
function toggle_innerdiv(){
var innerdiv=document.getElementById
("innerdiv");
```

```
if (innerdiv.style.visibility=="visible") {
    innerdiv.style.visibility= "hidden";
  } else {
    innerdiv.style.visibility= "visible";
}
}
```

Figure 7-5 shows an example of change in the visibility properties. The outer **div** is made hidden, and the inner **div** is made visible.

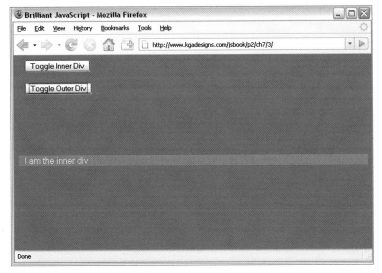

Figure 7-5 Visibility is toggled

Smart entry

Auto fill, auto suggest, intellisense: these are some terms used for the functionality of having words suggested to choose from as you type into a text box. In this example, the names of countries are used to draw from. As entry is made, each keystroke – when the key comes up (the `onkeyup` event) – runs a function that looks for country name matches based on what is in the entry box. As the entry continues, letter for letter, the suggested list gets smaller, perhaps becoming empty if suggested matches can no longer be made.

Considering there are many countries, this example limits the choices to just countries that start with A, B or C. Figure 7-6 shows a web page with a text box. One letter so far, B, has been entered, and the `textarea` below has filled up with suggested countries that start with B.

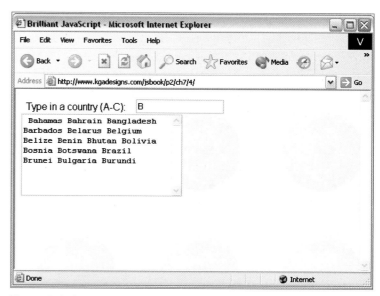

Figure 7-6 Countries are suggested based on the entry

As another letter is entered, the suggestions adjust accordingly, as seen in Figure 7-7.

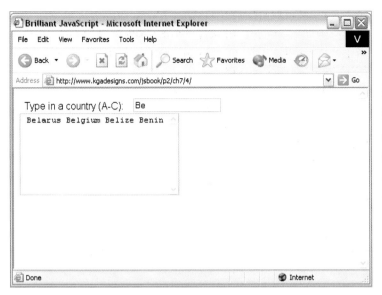

Figure 7-7 The suggestions filter to the entry

The list of suggestions updates upon each letter being entered. This occurs because the `onkeyup` event calls the `get_list` function. This function compares the entry with the list of countries stored in an array. The test for the match occurs in a loop that compares the entry with the full list of countries. Any that match are passed to the `value` property of the larger box, a `textarea` named `countrylist`. This box is always cleared first. Listing 7-4 shows the complete code.

Listing 7-4 Suggestions based on entry

```
<html>
<head>
<title>Brilliant JavaScript</title>
<style>
td {font-weight:bold;text-align:right;}
body {background-
image:url('globe1.jpg');color:black;font-
family:Arial}
</style>
<script type="text/javascript">
function clear() {
```

Smart entry (cont.)

```javascript
      document.getElementById("country
      list").value="";
      document.getElementById("txtEntry").
      value="";
}
function get_list() {
   entrybox=document.getElementById
   ("txtEntry");
   entry_value=entrybox.value.toUpper Case();
   list=document.getElementById
   ("countrylist");
   list.value="";
   var countries = new
Array("Afghanistan","Albania","Algeria","And
orra","Angola","Antigua","Argentina","Armeni
a","Australia","Austria","Azerbaijan","Baham
as","Bahrain","Bangladesh","Barbados","Belar
us","Belgium","Belize","Benin","Bhutan","Bol
ivia","Bosnia","Botswana","Brazil","Brunei",
"Bulgaria","Burundi","Cambodia","Cameroon","
Canada","Cape_Verde","Chad","Chile","China",
"Colombia","Comoros","Congo","Costa_Rica","C
roatia","Cuba","Cyprus","Czech_Republic");
   for (i=0;i<countries.length;i++) {
      if (countries[i].toUpperCase().
      indexOf(entry_value,0)==0) {
         list.value=list.value + " " +
         countries[i];
      }
   }
}
function fill_box() {
 var txt = '';
 if (window.getSelection) {
    txt = window.getSelection().
    toString();
 }
 else if (document.getSelection) {
    txt = document.getSelection();
 }
 else if (document.selection) {
    txt = document.selection.create
    Range().text;
```

```
    }
    else return;
    entrybox=document.getElementById
    ("txtEntry");
    entrybox.value=txt;
}
</script>
</head>
<body onload="clear()">
<form id="myform" action="#">
  Type in a country (A-C):
  
<input type="text" id="txtEntry"
onkeyup="get_list()" />
<br />
<textarea rows="8" cols="30"
id="countrylist" ondblclick="fill_box()"
></textarea>
</form>
</body>
</html>
```

The example has two functions: **get_list** which fills the
textarea box with suggestions based on the entry, and
fill_box which fills the text entry box with any country
name that is double-clicked in the **textarea** box. In other
words, entry is made in the standard text box and the larger
textarea updates with suggestions. Once a desired
suggestion is found, double-clicking on it will put it in the text
box, effectively completing the entry.

For your information

The **toUpperCase**
method is applied to the
entry and the list of
countries as they are cycled
through. This technique
removes any case sensitivity.
All comparisons are made in
the same upper case.

Smart entry (cont.)

For your information

There are more efficient variations of this technique. The way it is presented here is to demonstrate both the `onkeyup` and the `ondblclick` events.

Figure 7-8 shows that Belgium was double-clicked and placed in the text box.

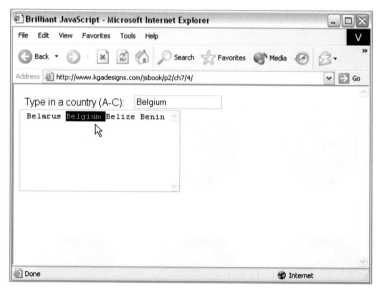

Figure 7-8 A suggested country is placed in the text box by double-clicking

It is common to tab through a form. Often it is difficult to see which box, button, menu, etc. of the form has the focus. Not any more. This example shows how to highlight the text box that has the focus. In step with this, it is also necessary to remove the highlighting from a text box that no longer has the focus. Two complementary events – `onfocus` and `onblur` – are used for this very need.

Figure 7-9 shows an entry form with three boxes. As each is tabbed or clicked into, the label to the left turns red. In Figure 7-9 the first name is being entered, and the label indicates that text box has the focus.

Figure 7-9 Highlighting the label to easily identify where the entry is going

Each label is in a `<span></span>` tag. As each text box is entered, the `onfocus` event calls the `highlight_on` function – passing it the `id` of the particular `span` tag. The function changes the style of the span such that the text changes to red. Conversely when the text box is exited, the `highlight_off` function is called with the `onblur` event, and the function returns the label's text colour back to black.

Highlighting where the entry is going

For your information

This example demonstrates the `onfocus` and `onblur` events.

Jargon buster

The `onblur` event has nothing to do with something visual actually getting blurry. It is simply a complementary opposite of something that gets the focus. Makes sense? I hope. I kept expecting to see some image get blurry when I first learned about this!

Highlighting where the entry is going (cont.)

Listing 7-5 shows the script of this example. Note that in the HTML portion, the labels are inside **span** tags, and each **span** tag has a unique **id** which is used in the event call.

Listing 7-5 Getting focused, getting blurred

```html
<html>
<head>
<title>Brilliant JavaScript</title>
<style>
td {font-weight:bold;text-align:right;}
body {background-
color:yellow;color:black;font-family:Arial}
</style>
<script type="text/javascript">
function highlight_on(spanname) {
 var s= document.getElementById (spanname)
   s.style.color="red";
}
function highlight_off(spanname) {
 var s= document.getElementById (spanname)
   s.style.color="black";
}
</script>
</head>
<body>
<form id="myform" action="" onsubmit="return
checkform()">
<table>
<tr><td><span id="firstname">Enter your
first name</span></td>
<td><input type="text" id="First"
onfocus='highlight_on("firstname")'
   onblur='highlight_off("firstname")'
   /></td></tr>
<tr><td><span id="lastname">Enter your last
name</span></td>
<td><input type="text" id="Last"
onfocus='highlight_on("lastname")'
   onblur='highlight_off("lastname")'
   /></td></tr>
<tr><td><span id="address">Enter your
address</span></td>
```

```
<td><input type="text" id="Addr"
onfocus='highlight_on("address")'
    onblur='highlight_off("address")'
    /></td></tr>
</table>
</form>
</body>
</html>
```

**Highlighting
where the entry
is going (cont.)**

7

Enhancing the web page

Introduction

Adding a little spice, a splash of pizzazz, will make your web pages more fun to use. In the world of search engine optimisation and analytical reporting on website usage, a bit of 'stickiness' is helpful. That is, if the web page is catchy, a viewer may stick around longer; and up go the statistics. What could be better than that?

What you'll do

Keep track of how long a page has been open

Use a quick print button

Incorporate a font size selector

Select text and background colours from a hidden palette

Did you know?

Personalisation

It's human nature to gravitate to the familiar. In web land, personalisation can be handled in a few different ways. The most comprehensive ability to personalise a web page is when user preferences are stored in a database. Then, whenever the person visits the site, and presumably logs in, all the likes the person has indicated can be put on the page.

The next method is saving preference data in cookies. This has merit but is a little more dicey. At any time a person can turn cookies off, or more likely clean out the cookies and temporary files from their computer. Also, cookies don't follow a person if they use a different computer. If you have more than one computer, you may have had the experience of a web page 'remembering you' when you use one computer but not the other.

This chapter doesn't go into the detail of these methods but nonetheless offers a few customisation techniques to enhance the experience.

Keeping track of time spent on a web page

It's not uncommon to have a web page display a clock. Having the time directly in front of you may keep you aware of how long you've been staring at whatever is on that page in front of you. One step better is a counter that tells you how long you have been on the page. No guessing here. With a clock you have to remember what time you started. With a time elapsed counter, you know how long you have been on the web page.

Figure 8-1 shows a web page that displays the start time and how much time has passed since then, in minutes. The start time does not change; the count in minutes updates every second. In practical use, this might be less intrusive on the page, but it's rather bold here for the purpose of demonstration.

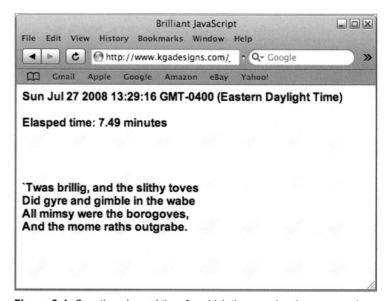

Figure 8-1 Counting elapsed time for which the page has been opened

The counter starts when the page is loaded or refreshed. Therefore any action that refreshes the page will restart the count, as well as state the new start time.

The fact that the counter is constantly updating must mean there is a timer function somewhere in play. The `setInterval` function handles the counter update, once per second. The function takes two parameters: a function to call, and the frequency of how often to call the function. The frequency is in milliseconds, so a setting of 1000 equals one second. Listing 8-1 lists the full code with a listing of the event sequences following.

Listing 8-1 Using a timing function to track elapsed time

```
<html>
<head>
<title>Brilliant JavaScript</title>
<style>
body {background-
image:url('back5.jpg');color:black;font-
family:Arial;font-weight:bold;}
</style>
<script type="text/javascript">
function start_time() {
  var start = new Date();
  document.getElementById("st").inner HTML=
  start;
}
function what_time() {
 var start=document.getElementById
 ("st").innerHTML;
 var counter=document.getElementById
 ("counter");
 var d2=Date.parse(start)
 var d= new Date();
 elapsed=((d-d2)/1000);
 counter.innerHTML="Elasped time: " +
 (elapsed/60).toFixed(2) + " minutes";
}
setInterval("what_time()",1000);
</script>
</head>
<body onload="start_time()";>
<div id="st">
</div>
<br />
<div id="counter">
</div>
<br /><br /><br /><br />
`Twas brillig, and the slithy toves<br />
Did gyre and gimble in the wabe<br />
All mimsy were the borogoves,<br />
```

8

```
And the mome raths outgrabe.<br />
</body>
</html>
```

Within the script block are two functions: `start_time` and `what_time`. Since these are functions they do not automatically run when the page is loaded. The `start_time` function does effectively run at the page load, as it is called in the load event:

```
<body onload="start_time()";>
```

Also, at the bottom of the script line is a single line that also runs at load time since it is not inside one of the functions:

```
setInterval("what_time()",1000);
```

What occurs then when the page loads is that the `start_time` function runs just once and populates the `st` div in the body with the start time. This stays constant and is not updated. The `setInterval` function sets up a timer event to fire each second, and what it does is run the `what_time` function. In this function a variable, `start`, gets the fixed start time from the `st` div. Another variable, `counter`, is populated with the 'at the moment' date/time. The `parse` method is used to convert the textual start time into a real time variable. The elapsed time is calculated as simply the new time minus the start time. Since this time-based maths returns a number of milliseconds, the difference of time is divided by 1000 to bring it up to seconds:

```
var start=document.getElementById("st").
innerHTML;
var counter=document.getElementById
("counter");
var d2=Date.parse(start)
var d= new Date();
elapsed=((d-d2)/1000);
```

Those with a sharp maths-minded brain might have concluded that the decimal part of the elapsed minutes runs to .99 before resetting to 0 and increasing the minutes by 1. The decimal part does not display seconds; it displays the percentage of a minute.

Finally, the `counter` div is updated with the new elapsed count, which is converted to minutes by being divided by 60:

```
counter.innerHTML="Elasped time: " +
(elapsed/60).toFixed(2) + " minutes";
```

The elapsed time shown in minutes is rounded to two decimal places, and eureka, you can now keep track of how much time you are spending on a certain page.

The technique shown here can be quite handy in certain situations. For example, in the workplace someone may have sensitive information showing on the screen. If for some reason they leave their desk, the timer could be tested for a certain elapsed time – 5 minutes, for example – and then close the browser.

8

Providing a print button

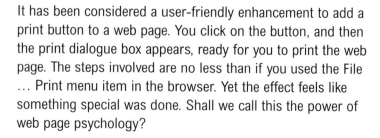

It has been considered a user-friendly enhancement to add a print button to a web page. You click on the button, and then the print dialogue box appears, ready for you to print the web page. The steps involved are no less than if you used the File … Print menu item in the browser. Yet the effect feels like something special was done. Shall we call this the power of web page psychology?

The fact is that it is not technically possible, and probably would be a security issue, to let the printer print without first displaying the print dialogue. Imagine if the printer would just print without any intervention after clicking the button on the page. It would be possible to have the printer print endlessly by accident (the button on the screen is enabled, and the Enter key is pressed down underneath a wad of papers).

Using a button to present the print dialogue takes merely a single line of code. Just put this within the button's tag and clicking the button will display the print dialogue:

```
onClick="javascript:window.print()"
```

Oops, forgot my spectacles. Darn, can't see the screen now. Yes you can! A neat feature to offer people viewing your site is the ability to change the font size to their liking. Figure 8-2 shows a web page with a famous quote on it. Underneath (although using CSS you can place this anywhere) are four links. Each one adjusts the size of the text.

Figure 8-2 Text can be resized

In Figure 8-2 the font size as shown is 12 points. This is an average size, and comfortable for most people. The Medium link, when clicked, set the text to 12 points. When it comes to viewing anything on a computer screen, though, what appears reasonable on one computer may not appear so on another, even with the same setting. A few factors affect this:

- the resolution of the computer screen
- the size of the monitor
- the density of the text (and any graphics), along with the contrast and colour scheme
- the distance the person sits from the computer screen
- the person's vision.

It's not surprising that word processors and other desktop applications have a zoom feature. Zoom settings help resolve issues with seeing items on the screen. Browsers also have a zoom-type feature. On most browsers, under the View menu are

Providing font resizing (cont.)

ways to grow or shrink the text, similar to this example. However, the advantage of building your own allows for better control.

Figure 8-3 shows how the page appears when the text is set to 10 points, by clicking the Small link.

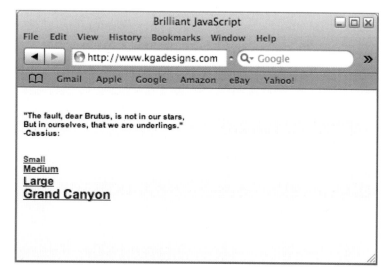

Figure 8-3 Text resized to 10 points

Note that although the text size changes, the sizes of the text links do not change. These values are fixed within **span** tags wrapping the links. Listing 8-2 shows the script, as well as the text and links that control the text size.

Listing 8-2 Script for resizing text

```
<html>
<head>
<title>Brilliant JavaScript</title>
<style>
body {font-family:arial;font-
weight:bold;background-color:#ffffcc}
</style>
<script type="text/javascript">
function resizetext(size) {
  switch (size) {
    case "10":
```

```
      alltext.style.fontSize = "10px";
      break;
    case "12":
      alltext.style.fontSize = "12px";
      break;
    case "14":
      alltext.style.fontSize = "14px";
      break;
    case "16":
      alltext.style.fontSize = "18px";
      break;
  }
}
</script>
</head>
<body id="alltext">
<br /><br />
"The fault, dear Brutus, is not in our
stars,<br />
But in ourselves, that we are underlings."
<br />
-Cassius:
<br /><br /><br />
<span style="font-size:10px;">
<a href="#" onclick="resizetext('10');return
false;">Small</a></span>
<br />
<span style="font-size:12px;">
<a href="#" onclick="resizetext('12');return
false;">Medium</a></span>
<br />
<span style="font-size:14px;">
<a href="#" onclick="resizetext('14');return
false;">Large</a></span>
<br />
<span style="font-size:16px;">
<a href="#" onclick="resizetext('16');return
false;">Grand Canyon</a></span>
</body>
</html>
```

8

Providing font resizing (cont.)

The key to this technique is to apply a style change to a section of the page. In this case, the change is applied to the `body` tag, thereby altering all text within. The `body` tag has an id, `alltext`:

```
<body id="alltext">
```

Each of the links calls the `resizetext` function, passing it a size as a parameter:

```
<span style="font-size:12px;">
<a href="#" onclick="resizetext('12');
return false;">Medium</a>
</span>
```

Note that the link is inside a `span` tag that keeps the link text set at 12 points. This prevents the links from being affected by the overall text resizing. The `resizetext` function simply applies the new text size to the `body`.

```
case "14":
    alltext.style.fontSize = "14px";
    break;
```

Figure 8-4 shows the Grand Canyon setting, named to convey LARGE text.

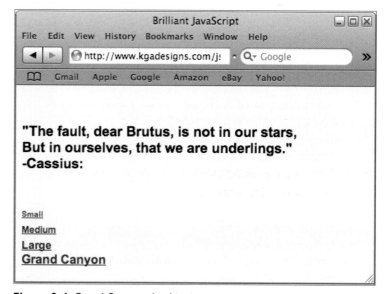

Figure 8-4 Grand Canyon-sized text

Going a step better than the browsers

As noted, browsers have built-in text resizing. Even so, with the technique presented so far you can still control the text size (or even other attributes – typeface, colour, etc.) to the degree that you need. Here now is a technique that the browsers can't compete with.

Using the technique, instead of applying it to the entire body, apply it to a section. Assuming there is a `div` section in your HTML code, the function can be pointed to work just on the `div`. The browsers cannot match this functionality because a browser has no way to customise its text sizing.

Figure 8-5 portrays this effect. The links used for the resizing are still on the page but control the sizing just in a section, in this case a `div` named `weather`.

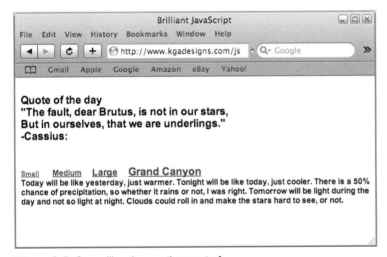

Figure 8-5 Controlling the weather, sort of

The coding is identical to that in Listing 8-2, except for two things. First, a `div` section with an id – `weather` – is in the page, and contains the weather report:

```
<div id="weather">
Today will be like yesterday, just warmer.
Tonight will be like today, just cooler.
There is a 50% chance of precipitation, so
```

Providing font resizing (cont.)

whether it rains or not, I was right. Tomorrow will be light during the day and not so light at night. Clouds could roll in and make the stars hard to see, or not.
</div>

Second, the function applies the resize to the **weather** div:

```
function resizetext(size) {
  switch (size) {
    case "10":
      weather.style.fontSize = "10px";
      break;
    case "12":
      weather.style.fontSize = "12px";
      break;
    case "14":
      weather.style.fontSize = "14px";
      break;
    case "16":
      weather.style.fontSize = "18px";
      break;
  }
}
```

In the same vein as applying a theme, this example shows how to apply a colour scheme. In this simple version just the page background colour and the body text colour are changeable. Figure 8-6 shows the page that is used to test colour schemes. Initially it is plain with some instructions, and a link in the top left – **change colors**.

Figure 8-6 A plain page to start

Clicking the **change colors** link toggles the visibility of the **palette** div. Inside this div are two colour palettes: one for the background, one for the text. Figure 8-7 shows the page with the **palette** div made visible.

See also

Toggling **div** sections is explained in Chapter 7.

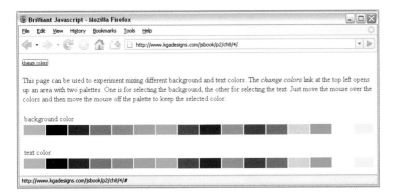

Figure 8-7 The colour palettes

The palettes are made from HTML tables, and each `<td>` tag has an **onmouseover** event that calls either the **backcolor** or **textcolor** function. Listing 8-3 shows the script.

Controlling page colours (cont.)

Listing 8-3 Choosing colours from palettes

```html
<html>
<head>
<title>Brilliant Javascript</title>
<style>
td {width:4%;}
</style>
<script type="text/javascript">
function backcolor(color) {
  document.body.style.backgroundColor =
  color;
}
function textcolor(color) {
  document.getElementById("alltext").
  style.color = color;
}
function toggle_palette(){
  var colors=document.getElementById
  ("colors");
  if (colors.style.visibility== "visible") {
      colors.style.visibility="hidden";
  } else {
      colors.style.visibility="visible";
  }
}
function initial_colors() {
  document.getElementById("colors").
  style.visibility="hidden";
}
</script>
</head>
<body id="alltext"
onload="initial_colors()">
<span style="font-size:10px;"><a href="#"
onclick="toggle_palette();return
false;">change colors</a></span>
<br /><br />
This page can be used to experiment mixing
different background and text colors. The
<i>change colors</i> link at the top left
```

opens up an area with two palettes. One is for selecting the background, the other for selecting the text. Just move the mouse over the colors and then move the mouse off the palette to keep the selected color.

```
<br />
<br />
<div id="colors">
<table>
<tr><td colspan="16">background
color</td></tr>
<tr>
<td style="background-color:aqua"
onmouseover="backcolor('aqua')">  </td>
<td style="background-color:black"
onmouseover="backcolor('black')"> 
</td>
<td style="background-color:blue"
onmouseover="backcolor('blue')">  </td>
<td style="background-color:fuchsia"
onmouseover="backcolor('fuchsia')"> </t
d>
<td style="background-color:gray"
onmouseover="backcolor('gray')">  </td>
<td style="background-color:green"
onmouseover="backcolor('green')"> 
</td>
<td style="background-color:lime"
onmouseover="backcolor('lime')">  </td>
<td style="background-color:maroon"
onmouseover="backcolor('maroon')"> </td
>
<td style="background-color:navy"
onmouseover="backcolor('navy')">  </td>
<td style="background-color:olive"
onmouseover="backcolor('olive')"> 
</td>
<td style="background-color:purple"
onmouseover="backcolor('purple')"> </td
>
```

8

Controlling page colours (cont.)

```html
<td style="background-color:red"
onmouseover="backcolor('red')">  </td>
<td style="background-color:silver"
onmouseover="backcolor('silver')"> </td
>
<td style="background-color:teal"
onmouseover="backcolor('teal')">  </td>
<td style="background-color:white"
onmouseover="backcolor('white')"> 
</td>
<td style="background-color:yellow"
onmouseover="backcolor('yellow')"> </td
>
</tr>
<tr><td colspan="16"> </td></tr>
<tr><td colspan="16">text color</td></tr>
<tr>
<td style="background-color:aqua"
onmouseover="textcolor('aqua')">  </td>
<td style="background-color:black"
onmouseover="textcolor('black')"> 
</td>
<td style="background-color:blue"
onmouseover="textcolor('blue')">  </td>
<td style="background-color:fuchsia"
onmouseover="textcolor('fuchsia')"> </t
d>
<td style="background-color:gray"
onmouseover="textcolor('gray')">  </td>
<td style="background-color:green"
onmouseover="textcolor('green')"> 
</td>
<td style="background-color:lime"
onmouseover="textcolor('lime')">  </td>
<td style="background-color:maroon"
onmouseover="textcolor('maroon')"> </td
>
<td style="background-color:navy"
onmouseover="textcolor('navy')">  </td>
<td style="background-color:olive"
onmouseover="textcolor('olive')"> 
```

```
</td>
<td style="background-color:purple"
onmouseover="textcolor('purple')"> </td
>
<td style="background-color:red"
onmouseover="textcolor('red')">  </td>
<td style="background-color:silver"
onmouseover="textcolor('silver')"> </td
>
<td style="background-color:teal"
onmouseover="textcolor('teal')">  </td>
<td style="background-color:white"
onmouseover="textcolor('white')"> 
</td>
<td style="background-color:yellow"
onmouseover="textcolor('yellow')"> </td
>
</tr>
</table>
</div>
</body>
</html>
```

The **backcolor** and **textcolor** functions handle applying the passed colour to the background colour of the **body**, or **alltext**, which is the id of the **body** tag:

```
function backcolor(color) {
    document.body.style.backgroundColor =
    color;
}
function textcolor(color) {
    document.getElementById("alltext").
    style.color = color;
}
```

Controlling page colours (cont.)

Figure 8.8 shows how the page appears after color choices have been made.

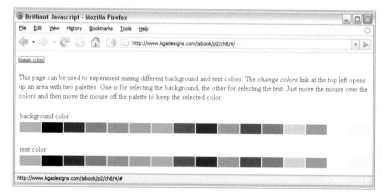

Figure 8-8 The page with a selected colour scheme

Working with text effects

Introduction

Web pages can show just two things: text and images. Whether viewing a plain page, a highly stylised page, or a page viewed with Flash or another plug-in, still all that you see are words and images. This chapter shows some tricks you can do with the words. The techniques in this chapter have been around since the dawn of the dynamic browser and have been used and abused for years. However, when applied sparingly within an overall design they can be quite effective. A page full of moving text that exists just to look cool no longer looks cool. Instead, defining an area on a page to apply some of the techniques works better. These examples don't guide you how and where to apply them. That would be part of your design. These examples do show you how to make them happen.

Stretching and contracting text

Watching text expand and contract is certainly an eye-catcher. The effect is possible by merely adding or removing space between letters or words. More space pushes letters away from each other – the stretch. Contracting is of course the opposite – removing space.

Figure 9-1 shows a message stretching across the page. Obviously the effect cannot be shown in a still picture, but Figure 9-2 shows the text during the contraction phase of the routine for comparison, drawing back into itself – contracting, in other words.

Figure 9-1 Text is being stretched

Figure 9-2 The text is contracting

So, how is this done? An array is set with pixel sizes ranging from −8 through 8, in steps of 2. The negative numbers are applied to contraction, and the positive numbers are used for stretching. A function, **animate**, is called periodically from the **setTimeout** function. The frequency is set with a variable named **delay**, initially set to 50 when the page loads. This value can be changed. A higher number creates a slower effect.

In the **animate** function a series of tests determines the current spacing factor and adjusts to the next one accordingly. Finally, the next spacing pixel amount is applied using the **letterSpacing** property. Listing 9-1 contains the full script. Note that in this example the script is in the body section of the page, after the **<p>** tag that contains the text. This is necessary so that the **<p>** tag, with the id of **stretch**, is recognised when the routine starts. The routine starts upon the page loading, since **animate** is called during the load.

Listing 9-1 Stretching and contracting text

```
<html>
<head>
<title>Brilliant JavaScript</title>
<style>
body {font-family:arial;font-
weight:bold;background-color:#eeeeff}
</style>
</head>
<body>
<br /><br /><br />
<p style="text-align:center;font-size:26px;"
id="stretch">Stretching is good for the
body</p>
<script type="text/javascript">
delay=50;
var space = new Array("-8px","-4px","-
2px","-1px","0px", "1px", "2px", "4px",
"8px");
space.pos = 0;
function animate() {
   var stretch = document.getElementById(
   "stretch");
```

Stretching and contracting text (cont.)

```
  if (stretch.direction==null) {
    stretch.direction = 1;
  }
  else if ((space.pos > space.length-2) ||
  (space.pos==0)) {
    stretch.direction *= -1;
  }
  stretch.style.letterSpacing =
  space[space.pos += stretch.direction];
 setTimeout('animate()',delay);
}
animate();
</script>
</body>
</html>
```

All browsers display a message in the title bar. This is the top of the browser – above any menus and toolbars. The displayed message will typically show the name of the browser if nothing else is indicated. The most often used way to place a useful message in the title bar is to have a `<title></title>` tag set in the HTML page code. Whatever is in the title tag appears in the browser title bar. Looking through the examples in this book, you will notice that throughout, the wording – Brilliant JavaScript – is always displayed, as that is within the title tags in every example.

Here is the one example where that message is overridden. In Listing 9-2 you can see that the HTML title is still 'Brilliant JavaScript', but the script overrides that with the 'All good things will come in time' message. Hmm, maybe this book is part JavaScript, part inspirational.

Listing 9-2 Scrolling a message in the title bar

```
<html>
<head>
<title>Brilliant JavaScript</title>
<style>
body {font-family:arial;font-
weight:bold;background-color:#eeeeff}
</style>
<script type="text/javascript">
var scrll = " All good things will come in
time ";
function scroller() {
  scrll = scrll.substring(1, scrll.length) +
  scrll.substring(0, 1);
  document.title = scrll;
  setTimeout("scroller()", 100);
}
</script>
</head>
<body onload="scroller()">
<br /><br />
Title bar scroll example
</body>
</html>
```

9

Whatever happened to scrolling in the status bar?

Did you know?

Whatever happened to scrolling in the status bar?

The status bar is the informational feedback section at the bottom of the browser. Older browsers provided a method to scroll text here as well. Newer browsers do not. The decision is one of practicality. The role of the status bar is to impart important information, such as errors, page loading problems and whatever else. Therefore the status bar should stay available at all times to the needs of the browser.

The displayed message is set into a variable:

```
var scrll = " All good things will come in time ";
```

The scroller function rotates the text at the speed of the interval used in the **setTimout** function. The title property of the document is where the message is placed.

```
function scroller() {
  scrll = scrll.substring(1, scrll.length) +
  scrll.substring(0, 1);
  document.title = scrll;
  setTimeout("scroller()", 100);
}
```

Since the advent of this technique so long ago, an interesting twist appeared when browsers began to support a multiple tab interface. Now the scrolling happens in the title bar, and in the tab heading, as shown in Figure 9-3.

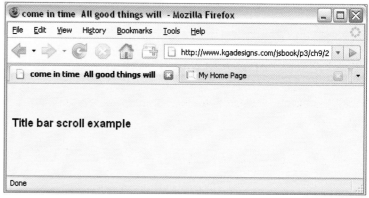

Figure 9-3 The scrolling text appears in the title bar and the tab heading

An eye-catching effect is to have the text on a button scroll. This could serve as an aid in directing the viewer to take action. In sales and marketing concerns, the key goal is to entice the customer to take action. This may or may not be sensible for your web page, but nonetheless it is another technique for your coding toolbox.

Figure 9-4 shows a button on a page that has scrolling text. The text scrolls upon the page load so the scrolling is live without any user intervention. With this approach the supposed 'call to action' is set up before the viewer has to take any action.

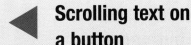
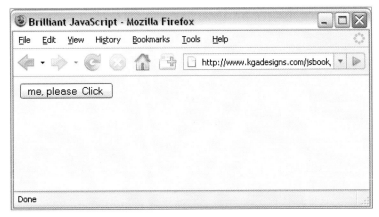

Figure 9-4 When the page loads, the button scrolls

When the button is clicked, the scrolling stops, as seen in Figure 9-5.

Figure 9-5 Once clicked, the scrolling stops

9

Scrolling text on a button (cont.)

Listing 9-3 shows the script. Within the script block are two functions: `button_scroll` and `button_clicked`. The `button_scroll` function is called when the page loads. It starts the scroll, and the `setTimeout` function within the `button_scroll` function calls the `button_scroll` function at a regular interval:

```
timeoutID = setTimeout("button_
scroll()",scroll_speed);
```

Note that a variable, `timeoutID`, is set to the `setTimeout` function. When the button is clicked, the `onclick` event of the button calls the `button_clicked` function; and it is in this function that the `timeoutID` variable is used.

The `button_clicked` function uses the `clearTimeout` function to stop the repetitiveness of the scrolling. This is possible because the `timeoutID` variable is used in the `clearTimeout` function. By passing the variable to the `clearTimeout` function, the scrolling stops. Then the text on the button is changed to 'I have been clicked':

```
function button_clicked() {
    window.clearTimeout(timeoutID);
    document.getElementById("mybutton").
    value="I have been clicked";
}
```

Listing 9-3 Scrolling text in a button

```
<html>
<head>
<title>Brilliant JavaScript</title>
<style>
body {font-family:arial;font-
weight:bold;background-color:#eeeeff}
</style>
</head>
<body>
<form>
<input type="button" id="mybutton"
value="Click me, please"
        onclick="button_clicked()" />
```

```
</form>
<script type="text/javascript">
var scroll_text=" Click me, please ";
var scroll_speed=100;
var scroll_count=0;
function button_scroll(){
  var btn=document.getElementById
  ("mybutton");
  scroll_text = scroll_text.substring(1,
  scroll_text.length)
  + scroll_text.substring(0, 1);
  btn.value=scroll_text;
  timeoutID = setTimeout("button_scroll()",
  scroll_speed);
}
function button_clicked() {
  window.clearTimeout(timeoutID);
  document.getElementById("mybutton").
  value="I have been clicked";
}
button_scroll();
</script>
</body>
</html>
```

For your information

In this example, the script block is placed in the body, after the button reference in the HTML code. Since the scrolling starts immediately, the button must already be a rendered page item before any code attempts to address it.

The `button_clicked` function that stops the scroll could and should do more. As it is, this demonstrates that the click of the button is captured and the scrolling stops. But then what? In your applications, this is where pertinent activity would be initiated.

9

Displaying text, typewriter style

A page renders in the browser, the text appears in one fell swoop, and on to the reading of it you go. Or, as shown previously in this chapter, text might scroll for a catchy effect. This example shows another effect, unofficially known as the typewriter: displaying text character by character at the speed someone might be typing.

Figure 9-6 shows a page in which a `textarea` box is being filled in the typewriter fashion. The effect is catchy as you wait to see what will show next. This is especially so when the source text is not known. Many news reporting sites use this technique to display the latest stories.

Figure 9-6 A box slowly fills up with text

Listing 9-4 shows the script that works this magic. It is fairly simple to implement. A variable, `poem` in this example, is set to the text. The `typewriter` function contains code that cycles through the text character by character.

Listing 9-4 The typewriter effect

```
<html>
<head>
<title>Brilliant JavaScript</title>
<style>
body {font-family:arial;font-
weight:bold;background-color:#ffeeff}
</style>
<script type="text/javascript">
```

```
var pos = 0
var poem= "There is another sky, Ever
serene and fair," +
    "And there is another sunshine, Though
    it be darkness there; " +
    "Never mind faded forests, Austin, Never
    mind silent fields - " +
    "Here is a little forest, Whose leaf is
    ever green;"
function typewriter() {
  var poem_length = poem.length;
  document.myform.mytextarea.value =
  document.myform.mytextarea.value +
          poem.charAt(pos);
  pos++;
  var timeID=  setTimeout("typewriter
  ()",80);
  if (pos >= poem_length) {
    clearTimeout(timeID); pos=0; }
}
</script>
</head>
<body onLoad= "typewriter()">
<form name="myform">
<textarea rows="6" cols="57"
name="mytextarea"></textarea>
</form>
</body>
</html>
```

The variable **pos** keeps the position where in the text the next character to display is found. The text is written into the **mytextarea** text area.

For your information

Throughout much of the book, the **getElementById** method has been used to provide a handle to a screen element. In this example another method is used to focus on the **textarea** control. This construct follows the document.form.control syntax, and in this example is seen as **document.myform. mytextarea.**

9

Generating random text

Random text generation is like a recipe. Create a random number; create an array of text strings. Mix the two together and the result is a random text string.

Listing 9-5 shows the script that provides random messages. An array is created to hold the messages, and a random number that is no larger than the number of array elements is used as the element index number to select which text is written out. Each time the page is loaded or refreshed, the random number refreshes to an unknown number, thereby ensuring the variety of messages gets displayed in no particular order.

Listing 9-5 Random wisdom

```
<html>
<head>
<title>Brilliant JavaScript</title>
<style>
body {font-family:arial;font-
weight:bold;background-color:#ffeeff}
</style>
<script type="text/javascript">
var wisdom = new Array;
wisdom[0]="The secret of success is to do
common things uncommonly
well.";
wisdom[1]="Every man dies; not every man
really lives";
wisdom[2]="Go out on a limb, you might like
the view";
wisdom[3]="The saddest moment in a person's
life comes but once";
wisdom[4]="A wolf in sheep's clothing needs
professional help";
wisdom[5]="Never cut what you can untie";
wisdom[6]="There are too many sad things in
this world. Don't walk
away from the happy ones";
wisdom[7]="The first step in getting out of
a hole, is to stop
digging";
wisdom[8]="Why is the time of day with the
```

```
slowest traffic called
rush hour?";
wisdom[9]="Worry gives a small thing a big
shadow";
wisdom[10]="One of the advantages of being
disorderly is that one is
constantly making exciting discoveries";
wisdom[11]="Falsehood is easy, truth so
difficult";
wisdom[12]="You can observe a lot just by
watching.";
wisdom_count = wisdom.length-1;
document.write(wisdom[Math.round(Math.random
()*(wisdom_count))]);
</script>
</head>
<body>
</body>
</html>
```

Figure 9-7 shows one of the random messages displayed in the browser.

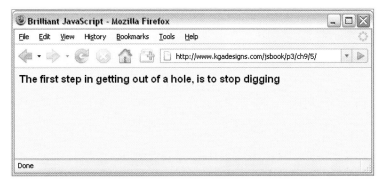

Figure 9-7 Random wisdom

Working with images

10

Introduction

There's no denying that imagery is intertwined with the websites we all visit. Pictures really do speak volumes when all the space a website gets to intrigue you is no larger than the size of a small television. And even a small television provides moving images. So it's no surprise that a lot of muscle has been put into what web pages can do with graphics.

What you'll do

Preload images and create image rollovers

Use a scrollable photograph marquee

Use a technique to quickly zoom in on an image, and return it to size

Preloading images

Right from the get-go, the managing of web graphics can take place before you even see them! This technique, known as preloading, gets the image files off the web server and into the browser in the fastest, most efficient way. It is not all that complicated. What preloading does is get the images into the cache of the browser before the page renders in the browser. The point is that when the page appears, the images appear instantly along with the rest of the page.

Browsers take advantage of the cache to store page elements that do not change. So when a page is loaded again, another time, the browser could be set to check the cache first to present the page. Using the cache is determined in the options or preferences settings, with some type of question about whether to always look for the latest version of web pages – yes or no. When no is selected, the browser attempts to display a page from memory. This is often a bad choice as the web is dynamic. For example, what if on Saturday you navigate to your favourite news site and are shown the news from last Thursday? Not good. So most browsers are kept on the setting to always get a full new page every time a page is loaded. Actually there is a happy medium. The browser will work from the cache and update just the items that are new.

With preloading, the cache is where images are placed to be ready to present with the rest of the page. But this doesn't happen on its own. This is coded in.

The procedure is simple. A new image object is created, and passed the path (or URL) to the image. The script must be in the head section as it has to run before any part of the HTML body is rendered. Listing 10-1 shows how this is coded.

Jargon buster

The **cache** (pronounced 'cash') is a temporary memory location.

Listing 10-1 Preloading images

```
<script type="text/javascript">
    fruit_on= new Image(120,120);
    fruit_on.src="apples.jpg";
    fruit_off= new Image(120,120);
    fruit_off.src="oranges.jpg";
    animal_on= new Image(120,120);
```

```
        animal_on.src="dog.jpg";
        animal_off= new Image(120,120);
        animal_off.src="cat.jpg";
    </script>
```

Preloading images is often used in conjunction with image rollovers, which are discussed next. With that in mind, the above code snippet is the structure for preloading two sets of images. Four images are preloaded: two fruit images and two animal images. Taking one image for an example, `fruit_on` is a variable assigned to an instance of the `Image` object. Also, within the instantiation, the dimensions of the image are established (120 × 120). The `fruit_on` variable at this moment is a placeholder that is holding nothing. The next line sets a real image to the variable: `fruit_on.src="apples.jpg";`.

In this example, `apples.jpg` must be in the same directory as the web page itself since there is no path preceding the file name.

Rollovers involve two images, an 'on' image and an 'off' image. For this reason images are preloaded in pairs.

10

Image rollovers

Image rollovers work with the movement of the mouse. Initially the 'off' image is presented, since initially the mouse is off the image. When the mouse is over the image, the 'on' image is shown. Figure 10-1 shows the initial state of the page after loading. Two images are shown, both being the 'off' images.

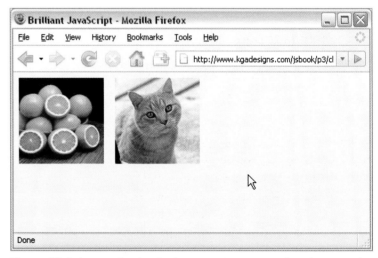

Figure 10-1 A page showing the images set to appear when the mouse is not over the pictures

The oranges and the cat respectively are the 'off' images. When the mouse is moved over the oranges, the image is replaced with one of apples, shown in Figure 10-2.

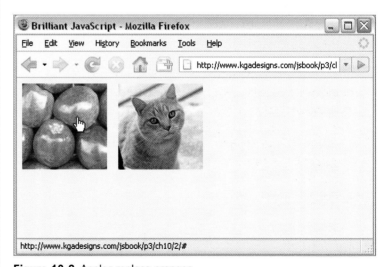

Figure 10-2 Apples replace oranges

Listing 10-2 contains the full page and script code. Listing 10-1 showed just the script. The full page of code provides a clearer understanding of how the images change.

Listing 10-2 Image rollover functionality

```
<html>
<head>
<title>Brilliant JavaScript</title>
<style>
body {font-family:arial;font-
weight:bold;background-color:#eeeeff}
</style>
<script type="text/javascript">
    fruit_on= new Image(120,120);
    fruit_on.src="apples.jpg";
    fruit_off= new Image(120,120);
    fruit_off.src="oranges.jpg";
    animal_on= new Image(120,120);
    animal_on.src="dog.jpg";
    animal_off= new Image(120,120);
    animal_off.src="cat.jpg";
</script>
</head>
<body>
<a href="#" onmouseover="javascript:
document.fruit.src='apples.jpg'"
    onmouseout="javascript:document.
    fruit.src='oranges.jpg'">
<img src="oranges.jpg" name="fruit"
border="0"></a>
  
<a href="#" onmouseover="javascript:
document.animal.src='dog.jpg'"
    onmouseout="javascript:document.
    animal.src='cat.jpg'">
<img src="cat.jpg" name="animal"
border="0"></a>
</body>
</html>
```

10

Image rollovers (cont.)

Each rollover action is handled in a long anchor tag `<a></a>`:

```
<a href="#" onmouseover="javascript:
document.animal.src='dog.jpg'"
    onmouseout="javascript:document.
    animal.src='cat.jpg'">
<img src="cat.jpg" name="animal"
border="0"></a>
```

The anchor tag contains the typical `href` to create a hyperlink. This is not necessary – rolled-over images do not have to be hyperlinks but commonly are. In this example the link is set to just keep the same page presented, so, `href="#"`.

The last part of the anchor tag displays the initial image. Here, with an `<img` tag, the `src` attribute is set to the 'off' picture, `cat.jpg`. When the mouse is moved over the image, the `onmouseover` event calls an inline JavaScript routine to change the image to `dog.jpg`. This is accomplished by using the document object and the named subsection – `animal`. Note that `animal` is the name used initially in the `<img` tag that presented the cat image. Following the `onmouseover` event, the `onmouseout` event uses JavaScript to reverse the image back to the cat – the 'off' picture.

For your information

It is possible to have a three-image process. The initial image is presented before any mouse activity is used. The image reverts to the cat image because that is the image file referenced in the `onmouseoff` event. This event could reference a different image. The effect then would be that the page loads with an initial image that is never seen again once the mouse moves over it – because when the mouse moves off, the secondary 'off', image is presented.

To wrap this up, Figure 10-3 shows the dog that appears when the mouse goes over the cat image. Dogs, cats, mice – all working together – only in computer land.

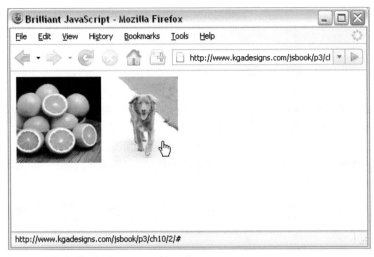

Figure 10-3 Replacing a cat with a dog

Showcasing photographs in a marquee

The photo album has come and gone as the best way to keep your memories. If you look at any tarnished and yellowed old photographs you have, and then compare these with the digital photographs of today – which give a better presentation?

The great attribute of digital photographs is that you can place them on a web page. Well, nothing new there. That has been part and parcel for a long time.

Having a series of photographs move in an animated fashion is a different thing altogether. With a custom photo marquee, you can showcase your best photos for the world to see. For this demonstration I assembled several photographs of rainbows I've collected over time. Some are the typical ones seen in the sky, and a few are ones that are always present at Niagara Falls. Figure 10-4 is a screen capture taken as these gems are scrolling by.

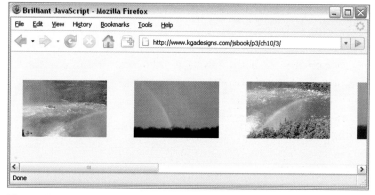

Figure 10-4 Moving photographs, figuratively and literally

The routine that performs this quasi-slide show is a bit lengthy. Listing 10-3 shows the complete page and JavaScript code, followed by some highlights on what makes it tick.

Listing 10-3 It's a slide show, it's a marquee, it's cool, whatever you want to call it

```
<html>
<head>
<title>Brilliant JavaScript</title>
<style>
```

```
body {font-family:arial;font-
weight:bold;background-color:#eeeeff}
</style>
<script type="text/javascript">
var images = new Array;
function image_link(name, width, link){
     this.name = name
     this.width = width
     this.link = link
}
images[0] = new image_link('rainbow1.
jpg',200,'rainbow1.jpg');
images[1] = new image_link('rainbow2.
jpg',200,'rainbow2.jpg');
images[2] = new image_link('rainbow3.
jpg',200,'rainbow3.jpg');
images[3] = new image_link('rainbow4.
jpg',200,'rainbow4.jpg');
images[4] = new image_link('rainbow5.
jpg',200,'rainbow5.jpg');
images[5] = new image_link('rainbow6.
jpg',200,'rainbow6.jpg');
images[6] = new image_link('rainbow7.
jpg',200,'rainbow7.jpg');
images[7] = new image_link('rainbow8.
jpg',200,'rainbow8.jpg');
var speed = 20
var image_count = images.length
var interval
var imgArray = new Array(image_count)
var shuffle = new Array(image_count)
for (i=0;i<image_count;i++){
imgArray[i] = new Image()
imgArray[i].src = images[i].name
imgArray[i].width = images[i].width
a=0
   for (b=0;b<i;b++){
      a=a+images[b].width
   }
     shuffle[i] = a
   }
function startScrolling(){
     window.clearInterval(pause)
```

Showcasing photographs in a marquee (cont.)

```
      interval = setInterval("autoScroll
      ()",speed)
}
function autoScroll(){
   for (i=0;i<image_count;i++){
    shuffle[i] = shuffle[i] - 1
     if (shuffle[i] == -(images[i].width)){
     a = 0
     for (b=0;b<image_count;b++){
        if (b!=i){
           a = a + images[b].width
             }
         }
      shuffle[i] = a
      }
      document.images[i].style.left =
      shuffle[i]
    }
}
function stop(){
   window.clearInterval(interval)
}
function go(){
   interval = setInterval("autoScroll
   ()",speed)
}
pause = setInterval("startScrolling()",1000)
</script>
<body bgcolor='#eeffff'>
<script>
for (i=0;i<image_count;i++){
document.write('<a href = ' + images[i].link
+' target="_blank" ><img space=0 hspace=0
vspace=0 border=0 height=100
style=position:absolute;top:50;left:' +
shuffle[i] + '; src=' + images[i].name + '
onMouseOver=stop() onMouseOut=go()></a>')
}
</script>
</body>
</html>
```

Running through the key points, each element of an array of images, named `images`, has an instance of a structure that holds three pieces of information: the name of the image file, the width it will display at in the marquee, and the file that will appear in a separate window when the image is clicked. By no surprise the file being displayed and the file that will be displayed separately are the same. When displayed in the separate window, the size constraints are not applied so a bigger image will appear, if the original size is bigger than the size constraints:

```
images[2] = new image_link('rainbow3.
jpg',200,'rainbow3.jpg');
```

The speed that the marquee moves at is set in this line. The lower the number, the faster the marquee moves: `var speed = 20`.

Two more arrays, `imgArray` and `shuffle`, are used to facilitate the photos repositioning back when they have scrolled out of view. A function, `stop`, will stop the scrolling and present whichever picture was clicked on in a separate window. A function named `go` restarts the scrolling.

Finally, it is a script block in the body of the page that displays the marquee. The `document.write` method is used to set the pictures as a hyperlink. The `onmouseover` and `onmouseout` events respectively call the `stop` and `go` functions.

10

Showcasing photographs in a marquee (cont.)

Figure 10-5 shows the result of clicking on a photograph, and having it appear true to size in a separate window.

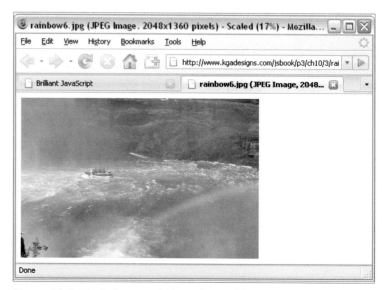

Figure 10-5 Displaying one photograph out of the marquee

In Chapter 8 a technique was shown that increases and/or decreases the font size. The technique shown in this example increases the size of an image. Often the method to do this is to click on a smaller image and have a larger file version of the same image open in a new window.

This technique is less cumbersome. On the web page are a couple of graphics. Simply clicking on them increases their size. Figure 10-6 shows the page.

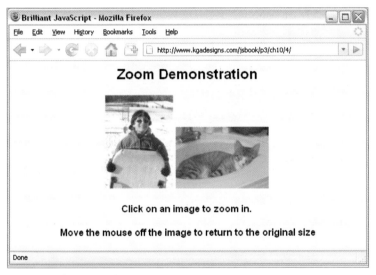

Figure 10-6 Images that can be zoomed

In the code, a variable, **`zoom_factor`**, stores the factor by which the image is increased. A value of 2 doubles the size. Listing 10-4 shows the script.

Listing 10-4 Getting all the detail with the zoom feature

```html
<html>
<head>
<title>Brilliant JavaScript</title>
<style>
body {text-align:center;font-
family:arial;font-weight:bold;background-
color:#eeecee}
</style>
```

Zooming in on an image (cont.)

```
<script type="text/javascript">
var zoom_factor = 2;
//width and height
var w;
var h;
// the original width and height
var start_width;
var start_height;
var clicks=0;
function zoom_in(img) {
 // curr_Img = this_Img;
  clicks++;
  if (clicks == 1) {
    start_width = img.width;
    start_height = img.height;
  }
   w = img.width;
   h = img.height;
   img.width = w * zoom_factor;
   img.height = h * zoom_factor;
}
function back_to_size(img) {
  if (clicks != 0) {
    img.width = start_width;
    img.height = start_height;
    clicks = 0;
 }
}
</script>
<body>
<h2>Zoom Demonstration</h2>
<img src="winterfun.jpg"
onclick="zoom_in(this)"
onmouseout="back_to_size(this)" />
<img src="sleepingcat.jpg"
onclick="zoom_in(this)"
onmouseout="back_to_size(this)" />
<br /><br />Click on an image to zoom in.
<br /><br />Move the mouse off the image to
return to the original size</p>
</body>
</html>
```

The original width and height are stored in the `start_width and start_height` variables. The count of mouse clicks is tracked as well. Each time an image is clicked, the image resizes up again by the `zoom_factor`. A few clicks and you have a very large image!

There are two functions running the show: `zoom_in` and `back_to_size`. The function for zooming in is triggered by a mouse click on the image, therefore giving the ability to keep track of the clicks. The `back_to_size` function is run whenever the mouse moves off the image, via the `onmouseout` event.

Figure 10-7 shows one of the images zoomed in. Notice that the mouse pointer remains on the image to keep it enlarged.

Figure 10-7 A zoomed-in image

Windows, pages, popups and prompts

Introduction

This chapter is about boxes. Outer boxes, and boxes in boxes. And boxes that won't go away until you make them do so. Let's get to the names. There are browser windows, pages, screens, popups, alerts, confirms and prompts. Generally speaking, the browser is a window, and it can open other windows. A page sits in a browser. The screen is what contains the browser. A popup is a window, usually designed to be on top of everything else. Alerts and prompts also sit on top and hold on to control of your browser until dismissed.

Did you know?

The problem with popups

Popups, which is a general term in the first place, have become synonymous with bad Internet behaviour. Popups contain ads, are annoying, pop up too often; they even pop under. That is, they will be sitting underneath the browser so when you close the browser – boom, there's the popup. Much virus software now will not display popups. I am not offering any solution to this problem, just pointing it out.

What you'll do

Write text and HTML tags to the browser

Learn how alerts, confirms and prompts work

Open new windows on existing URLs

Open a blank new window and write content to it

Dynamically resize an image based on the browser width

Writing content to the browser

The basic method to get content into the browser window is to use the **write** method of the **document** object. This method has been used throughout the book – it is the old tried and true workhorse for output.

The interesting thing about **document.write** is that since it outputs to the browser window, and the window recognises HTML code, therefore **document.write** can output formatting, links, images and more.

Another method used is to set text to the **innerHTML** property for tags that have the property: **div**s and paragraphs (**<p>**).

Figure 11-1 Simple output

Let's start with basic output. Figure 11-1 shows output of (1) regular text, (2) an image, and (3) formatted text.

The output is created with the `document.write` construct. Listing 11-1 shows how.

Listing 11-1 Basic text and HTML tag output

```html
<html>
<head>
<title>Brilliant JavaScript</title>
<style>
body {font-family:arial;font-
weight:bold;background-color:#ffddee}
</style>
<script type="text/javascript">
   document.write ("Hello, I am regular old
   text, but I think a cat is following
   me!");
   document.write ("<br /><br />");
   document.write("<img src='cat1.jpg' />");
   document.write ("<br /><br />");
   document.write ("<h2>I am inside a
heading tag, do I look any larger?</h2>");
</script>
</head>
<body>
<p id="paragraph1"></p>
</body>
</html>
```

The first line of text is written as just that – plain text. The image and the wording underneath are written as HTML. For example, an `<img src` tag is written as the output of the `write` method.

Listing 11-2 is similar, other than the paragraph in the body; the `id` of `paragraph1` is to be given content as its `innerHTML` property.

Writing content to the browser (cont.)

Listing 11-2 Attempting to write to a paragraph's `innerHTML` property

```
<html>
<head>
<title>Brilliant JavaScript</title>
<style>
body {font-family:arial;font-
weight:bold;background-color:#ffddee}
</style>
<script type="text/javascript">
  document.write ("Hello, I am regular old
  text, but I think a cat is following
  me!");
  document.write ("<br /><br />");
  document.write("<img src='cat1.jpg' />");
  document.write ("<br /><br />");
  document.write ("<h2>I am inside a
  heading tag, do I look any
  larger?</h2>");
  document.write ("<br /><br />");
  document.getElementById("paragraph1").
  innerHTML="I am the first paragraph";
</script>
</head>
<body>
<p id="paragraph1"></p>
</body>
</html>
```

This is the line meant to write content using `innerHTML`:

```
document.getElementById("paragraph1").innerH
TML="I am the first paragraph";
```

This seems straightforward and yet produces the error shown in Figure 11-2.

Figure 11-2 An output error

Why did this error occur? There is nothing wrong with the line of code that addresses the **innerHTML** code. Instead, it is where the line is placed. As the page renders into the browser the problematic line attempts to write to the paragraph element, but sequentially; the rendering has not yet created the paragraph. The error occurs from attempting to place output into an element that doesn't yet exist.

Listing 11-3 shows a different arrangement of code. The line that addresses the **innerHTML** property is now situated in the body, after the paragraph has been rendered.

Listing 11-3 A different attempt to write to a paragraph's **innerHTML** property

```
<html>
<head>
<title>Brilliant JavaScript</title>
<style>
body {font-family:arial;font-
weight:bold;background-color:#ffddee}
</style>
<script type="text/javascript">
document.write ("Hello, I am regular old
text, but I think a cat is following me!");
document.write ("<br /><br />");
document.write("<img src='cat1.jpg' />");
```

```
document.write ("<br /><br />");
document.write ("<h2>I am inside a heading
tag, do I look any larger?</h2>");
</script>
</head>
<body>
<p id="paragraph1"></p>
<script>
document.getElementById("paragraph1").innerH
TML="I am the first paragraph";
</script>
</body>
</html>
```

Figure 11-3 shows the corrected output. Now, there are elements on the screen created by a script in the header and a script in the body. Such flexibility!

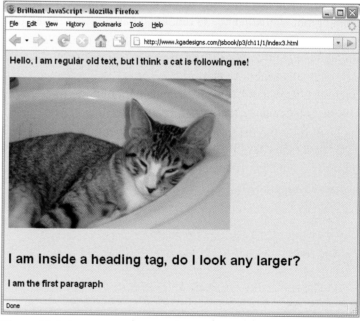

Figure 11-3 The output is corrected

The thing to remember is the sequencing of elements being rendered as the page loads. Until an element exists in the page, it cannot be addressed without causing an error. These next few lines are an alternative way to organise the code in Listing 11-3:

```
document.write ("<p id='paragraph1'>
</p>");
document.getElementById
("paragraph1").innerHTML="I am the first
paragraph";
</script>
</head>
<body>
</body>
</html>
```

The difference is that now **paragraph1** is not fixed in the body. Instead it is written dynamically and just before the line that addresses its **innerHTML** property. This works; the output is exactly the same as that produced by the code in Listing 11-3. The sequence is correct.

Listing 11-4 goes a step further. Now there is a table in the body section. JavaScript is used to change the text colour in the table. This works because the script that addresses the table text colour occurs in the body, after the table.

Listing 11-4 Using JavaScript to change all the cell text colouring in a table

```
<html>
<head>
<title>Brilliant JavaScript</title>
<style>
body {font-family:arial;font-
weight:bold;background-color:#ffddee}
</style>
<script type="text/javascript">
  document.write ("Hello, I am regular old
  text, but I think a cat is following
  me!");
  document.write ("<br /><br />");
  document.write("<img src='cat1.jpg' />");
```

```
document.write ("<br /><br />");
document.write ("<h2>I am inside a
heading tag, do I look any
larger?</h2>");
document.write ("<p id='paragraph1'>
</p>");
document.getElementById("paragraph1").
innerHTML="I am the first paragraph";
</script>
</head>
<body>
<table>
<tr><td>Cell 1</td><td><td>Cell 2</td></tr>
<tr><td>Cell 3</td><td><td>Cell 4</td></tr>
</table>
<script>
var cells= document.getElementsByTagName
("td");
  for (i=0;i<cells.length;i++) {
    cells[i].style.color="maroon";
  }
</script>
</body>
</html>
```

A useful method, **getElementsByTagName**, allows addressing all elements of a given type at once. In this case the **<td>** tag creates the cells in a table, gathered into an array named **cells**. The array is cycled through and the colour property is changed to maroon.

Figure 11-4 shows the final page of output. The table is near the bottom, no borders make it stand out, but the text from the cells is visible and in a different colour from the rest of the page text.

Timesaver tip

When necessary to address all elements of a given type, the **getElementsByTagName** is an instant way to gather the elements into a single array. The ids and/or names of individual elements do not matter.

Figure 11-4 Table cells are addressed together in one array

Alerts, prompts and confirms

In any computer-based application, communication is on the screen but is also supported by dialogue boxes. Some boxes give information, and some also accept input. In terms of JavaScript:

- An alert states a message.

- A prompt asks for input, which a person can decide to enter, or not, and still be able to dismiss the box.

- A confirm offers a choice response, OK or Cancel. These two choices are used loosely to gather a response that is yes or no, true or false, etc. The actual words OK and Cancel can't be changed but their purpose can be made clear by the message that appears in the confirm box.

Listing 11-5 shows code that runs through a sequence of using these dialogue-type boxes.

Listing 11-5 Prompts, alerts, questions, choices

```
<html>
<head>
<title>Brilliant JavaScript</title>
<style>
body {font-family:arial;font-
weight:bold;background-color:#eeeeff}
</style>
<script type="text/javascript">
var name= prompt("What is your name?","");
if (name!= null) {
    alert("Your name is " + name);
} else {
    alert ("No name was entered");
}
var doglover = confirm("Do you like dogs?");
if (doglover== true) {
    alert("Me too!");
} else {
    alert ("Dogs do tend to yap a lot");
}
</script>
</head>
```

```
<body>
</body>
</html>
```

The first action is that a prompt appears, asking for a name. Figure 11-5 shows the prompt.

Figure 11-5 Prompt for a name

With a prompt a number of results are possible:

■ A name is entered and the OK button is clicked.

■ A name is entered but the Cancel button is clicked.

■ The Cancel button is clicked without any input.

■ The OK button is clicked without any input.

Coding for all possibilities is a best practice. In this example, the code tests for which button was clicked. When Cancel is clicked, a null is returned, even if there is input. Conversely, clicking OK does not return a null, even if no entry was made. In this example no test is put in for an OK click with an empty entry. But no matter. All that will happen is that an alert will tell you your name is blank:

```
if (name!= null) {
    alert("Your name is " + name);
} else {
    alert ("No name was entered");
}
```

Figure 11-6 shows the alert box that displays after the prompt is dismissed. I am told my name is Ken. This example has the alert display the result from the prompt. Not useful in a real application. This is just reminding a person of what they just entered. Hopefully their attention span is a bit longer than that!

Alerts, prompts, and confirms (cont.)

Figure 11-6 Yes, my name is my name

A confirm box appears next. Regardless of what question is coded into it, the options are OK or Cancel. A question such as 'Do you like dogs?' is really a yes or no question, but OK and Cancel are displayed. If OK is clicked an alert appears, with the message 'Me too!' If Cancel is clicked the message is 'Dogs do tend to yap a lot'. Well, at least mine did – I used to hear him all the way down the block.

The `open` method of the `window` object is used to open a new browser window. There are a variety of factors affecting how this all works. The different browsers handle some of the commands in different ways. Also since browsers are now tabbed, it could be a new browser that is opened, or a new tab in the current browser. Yet the choice of a new browser or a new tab is not readily available. It depends on the browser settings. The consistency is not great among the different browsers. Enough said on that score. Figure 11-7 shows a page with three buttons. For convenience the operation that each button calls in the script is written next to the appropriate button. In particular, clicking a button calls a JavaScript function that has the exact line in it that is shown next to the button.

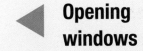

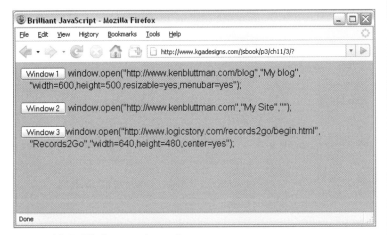

Figure 11-7 Window opening options

First, the basic syntax of the `open` method is
`window.open`(URL, window name, optional parameters).

The URL entry is just what it sounds like – the web address of what should appear in the new window. The window name serves no discernible purpose. It does not appear in or on the new window. The optional parameters are listed in Table 11-1.

Opening windows (cont.)

Table 11-1 Optional parameters of the `open` method

Option	Description
directories	Indicates whether the bookmarks toolbar should display in the new window
height	The height of the new window, in pixels
left	The distance from the left side of the screen where the new window will be placed, in pixels
location	Indicates whether the location bar is displayed in the new window
menubar	Indicates whether the menu bar is displayed in the new window
resizable	Indicates whether the new window can be resized
scrollbars	Indicates whether the new window can have scrollbars
status	Indicates whether the new window will have the status bar
toolbar	Indicates whether the new window will have the toolbar
top	The distance from the top of the screen where the new window will be placed, in pixels
width	The width of the new window, in pixels

Use of these options needs careful consideration. You may use them with the goal of keeping things simple for viewers, but taking away a menubar or a toolbar, or making the window non-resizable, might seem rather annoying. Sizing a window and taking away the scrollbars would make it hard for viewers to see any information not shown in the visible part of the window. So use these with restraint. Test the options in different browsers, on screens with different resolutions. If none of this is possible, I suggest you err on the side of caution and don't use many of these options.

Of the buttons seen in Figure 11-7, clicking on the first did indeed open my blog in a separate window, and it could be resized – see Figure 11-8.

Figure 11-8 A new window, set to an existing URL

Opening a new blank window

One advantage of opening a new window is to have one that is blank. That is – it is not set to an existing URL. This is accomplished simply by leaving the URL setting in the **open** method as an empty string (""). Then, you can use the **write** method to create content in the new window, as in Listing 11-6.

Listing 11-6 Creating a new window, with content

```
<html>
<head>
<title>Brilliant JavaScript</title>
<style>
body {font-family:arial;font-
weight:normal;background-color:#ee9eff}
</style>
<script type="text/javascript">
function window1() {
  var new_window=window.open("","A new
  window","");
  new_window.document.write("<html>
  <head><title>new</title></head>");
  new_window.document.write("<body
  style='background-color:lightblue'>");
  new_window.document.write("HELLO
  JUPITER!</body></html>");
  new_window.document.close();
}
</script>
</head>
<body>
<form>
<button id="button1"
onclick="window1()">Window 1</button>
</form>
</body>
</html>
```

A very useful and appreciated feature is to have your application provide content that fits the window of the viewer. Screen sizes and resolutions are in the hands of the viewer but luckily JavaScript can read dimensions about the screen and, more importantly, the browser.

Figure 11-9 shows an image. The image is sized, by width, to one-half of the browser, whether or not the browser is maximised or resized down. The image will always be one-half of the width.

Figure 11-9 The image width never exceeds half the browser width

The technique is simple: read the width of the browser, divide by 2, and set the image width to that number, shown here in Listing 11-7.

Listing 11-7 Calculating a dynamic width

```
<html>
<head>
<title>Brilliant JavaScript</title>
<style>
body {font-family:arial;font-
weight:bold;background-color:#eeeeff}
</style>
</head>
```

Planning for different screen sizes (cont.)

```
<body>
</body>
<script type="text/javascript">
if (window.innerWidth) {
  var w= window.innerWidth;
} else {
 w=document.body.clientWidth;
}
document.write("<img src='cat1.jpg' width='"
+
  (Math.round(w/2)).toString() + "' />");
</script>
</html>
```

Internet Explorer reports the browser width in a different manner, and this snippet accommodates Internet Explorer and the other browsers:

```
if (window.innerWidth) {
  var w= window.innerWidth;
} else {
  w=document.body.clientWidth;
}
```

Once the variable **w** has the browser width, the **write** method is used to dynamically place an **<img** tag, with a width setting of half the browser width.

Fancy and fun animation

Introduction

Pages and images that remain static cannot hold court with pages that change, morph or in some other way enhance the visual experience. Typically a page loads, the information is digested, the viewer moves on. OK, nothing wrong with that. But what about having them stick around a little bit longer? Give viewers something to sink their teeth in, or rather glue their eyeballs to.

This chapter shows some techniques to use, albeit sparingly for the best effect. Effects can be overdone, and restraint is just as important. A tease is good, a wallop of imagery is overwhelming. Effects can get stale over time, so a light touch is just right.

What you'll do

Apply page transitions

Create mouse trails

Bounce a ball around the screen and apply a number of parameters for control

Combine transitions with rollovers

Page transitions

A very common method in PowerPoint and KeyNote presentations is the transition between slides. There are many available effects when moving from one slide to the next, including Box in, Box out, Checkerboard across, Wipe left, Wipe down and Dissolve. These transition effects have real staying power when it comes to the 'ooh-aah' effect.

Transitions across web pages seem like a functionality that will grow in time. For now, without writing a rather lengthy custom script, the effect is available only in Internet Explorer. The effect is not an actual JavaScript routine, but is close enough in the page functions to be included here.

Figure 12-1 shows a transition under way. One page is being replaced by another but instead of a clean change, the new page is transitioned in.

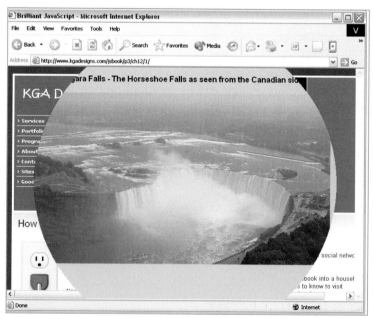

Figure 12-1 Transitioning between web pages

The changing of pages shown in Figure 12-1 is the Circle out transition. The transitions occur with the use of a meta tag. The syntax is thus:

```
<meta http-equiv="Page-Enter"
content="RevealTrans(Duration=4,
Transition=3)">
```

The meta tag line is placed in the page's head section.

Note that this occurs on a page enter (not the same as the load) event. The transition has to occur between two pages; the new page is being entered. Therefore the effect works when coming from a page one back in the history object, or entering the URL into the address bar. The effect will *not* occur when the browser is refreshed, as technically you are not entering the page at that point, just updating it.

Figure 12-2 shows the new page after the transition is complete,

Figure 12-2 The transition is complete

There are, as of this writing, 25 transitions, listed here in Table 12-1.

Page transitions
(cont.)

Table 12-1 Transitions available in Interner Explorer

Transition name	Meta tag code
Blend in	`<meta http-equiv="Page-Enter"content="blendTrans(Duration=4.0)">`
Box in	`<meta http-equiv="Page-Enter" content="RevealTrans(Duration=4,Transition=0)">`
Box out	`<meta http-equiv="Page-Enter" content="RevealTrans(Duration=4,Transition=1)">`
Circle in	`<meta http-equiv="Page-Enter" content="RevealTrans(Duration=4,Transition=2)">`
Circle out	`<meta http-equiv="Page-Enter" content="RevealTrans(Duration=4,Transition=3)">`
Wipe up	`<meta http-equiv="Page-Enter" content="RevealTrans(Duration=4,Transition=4)">`
Wipe down	`<meta http-equiv="Page-Enter" content="RevealTrans(Duration=4,Transition=5)">`
Wipe right	`<meta http-equiv="Page-Enter" content="RevealTrans(Duration=4,Transition=6)">`
Wipe left	`<meta http-equiv="Page-Enter" content="RevealTrans(Duration=4,Transition=7)">`
Vertical blinds	`<meta http-equiv="Page-Enter" content="RevealTrans(Duration=4,Transition=8)">`
Horizontal blinds	`<meta http-equiv="Page-Enter" content="RevealTrans(Duration=4,Transition=9)">`
Checkerboard across	`<meta http-equiv="Page-Enter" content="RevealTrans(Duration=4,Transition=10)">`
Checkerboard down	`<meta http-equiv="Page-Enter" content="RevealTrans(Duration=4,Transition=11)">`
Random dissolve	`<meta http-equiv="Page-Enter" content="RevealTrans(Duration=4,Transition=12)">`
Split vertical in	`<meta http-equiv="Page-Enter" content="RevealTrans(Duration=4,Transition=13)">`
Split vertical out	`<meta http-equiv="Page-Enter" content="RevealTrans(Duration=4,Transition=14)">`
Split horizontal in	`<meta http-equiv="Page-Enter" content="RevealTrans(Duration=4,Transition=15)">`

Split horizontal out	`<meta http-equiv="Page-Enter" content="RevealTrans(Duration=4,Transition=16)">`
Strips left down	`<meta http-equiv="Page-Enter" content="RevealTrans(Duration=4,Transition=17)">`
Strips left up	`<meta http-equiv="Page-Enter"content="Reveal Trans(Duration=4,Transition=18)">`
Strips right down	`<meta http-equiv="Page-Enter"content="Reveal Trans(Duration=4,Transition=19)">`
Strips right up	`<meta http-equiv="Page-Enter"content="Reveal Trans(Duration=4,Transition=20)">`
Random bars horizontal	`<meta http-equiv="Page-Enter" content="RevealTrans(Duration=4,Transition=21)">`
Random bars vertical	`<meta http-equiv="Page-Enter" content="RevealTrans(Duration=4,Transition=22)">`
Random	`<meta http-equiv="Page-Enter" content="RevealTrans(Duration=4,Transition=23)">`

12

Mouse trails

Mouse trails are after-images that follow the mouse pointer around the screen. There are many variations of this effect. Most mouse trails stop when the mouse movement is at rest. Other applications of this effect show spinning animation around the mouse pointer when it is not moving.

The version shown here takes a single graphic as the trailing image, and applies it as a series of images, with a gradual change of size. In other words, just one image becomes many. There could be other images if desired. For example there could be one image of each planet, and then the solar system could follow the mouse around. Here, it is one simple star, shown in Figure 12-3.

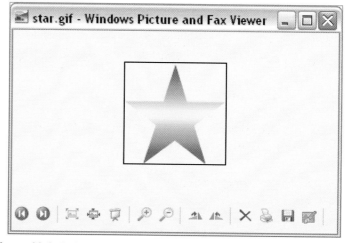

Figure 12-3 A simple graphic to use as the mouse trails

The speed at which the trailing images follow the mouse, and the distance between each image, are from settings in the code – and can be changed. Listing 12-1 shows the script.

Listing 12-1 Using a timing function to track elapsed time

```
<html>
<head>
<title>Brilliant JavaScript</title>
<style>
body {font-family:arial;font-
weight:bold;background-color:#eeeeff}
```

```
</style>
<script type="text/javascript">
layered=document.layers;
trails=new Array("star.gif",28,26,
"star.gif",m22,22,"star.gif",18,18,
    "star.gif",14,14,"star.gif",
    10,10,"star.gif",6,6)
var offsetx=15
var offsety=15
pageX=0;
pagey=0;
img_factor=parseInt(trails.length/3)
rate=30 //speed that mouse trails follow
mouse - lower number is faster
rightedge=window.innerWidth-trails[1]-20
bottomedge=window.pageYOffset+window.innerHe
ight-trails[2]
for (i=0;i<img_factor;i++){
createTrailBox("myDiv"+i,i*10,i*10,i*3+1,i*3
+2,"",
        "<img src='" + trails[i*3] + "'
        width=" + trails[(i*3+1)] +
        " height=" + trails[(i*3+2)] + "
        border=0>")
}
function createTrailBox(divname,x_pos,y_
pos,w,h,a,b,c,s){
 with (document){
  write("<div id='" + divname + "' "+"
  style='position:absolute;left:" +
      x_pos + "; top:" + y_pos + "; width:"+
      w +"; height:"+ h + "; ");
  write("'>");
  write(b);
  if (!c)
    write("</div>")
    write("</div>")
    }
  }
}
function get_x_pos(divname){
  return parseInt(document.getElementBy
  Id(divname).style.left)
}
```

Mouse trails (cont.)

```
function get_y_pos(divname) {
  return parseInt(document.getElementBy
  Id(divname).style.top)
}
function moveTrailBox(divname,DX,DY) {
  ddiv=document.getElementById(divname).
  style;
    rightedge=window.innerWidth-trails[1]-
    20;
    bottomedge=window.pageYOffset +
    window.innerHeight-trails[2];
  ddiv.left=Math.min(rightedge, DX +
  offsetx);
  ddiv.top=Math.min(bottomedge, DY +
  offsety);
}
function cycle() {
  for (i=0;i<(img_factor-1);i++) {
moveTrailBox("myDiv"+i,get_x_pos("myDiv"+(i+
1)),
get_y_pos("myDiv"+(i+1)))
  }
}
function newPos(e) {
  moveTrailBox("myDiv"+(img_factor-
  1),e.pageX + 2,e.pageY + 2)
}
document.onmousemove=newPos

setInterval("cycle()",rate)
</script>
</head>
<body>
<div id="startdiv"></div>
</body>
</html>
```

Here are some highlights of the script in Listing 12-1. An array is built with the star image, referencing it multiple times but with a different set of height and width settings:

```
trails=new Array("star.gif",28,26,"star.
gif",22,22,"star.gif",18,18,
    "star.gif",14,14,"star.gif",10,10,
    "star.gif",6,6)
```

The distance, horizontally and vertically, that the trails appear from the mouse pointer are:

```
var offsetx=15
var offsety=15
```

This next line calculates how many of the images will be visible. There is no correct number to use in this equation, as the number of images in the array is a variable. The number at the end, 3 in this example, is the number that can be changed for a different effect. The usefulness is that you can control how many of the images appear after the mouse pointer. Altering this number allows having less than the full array appear, if so desired:

```
img_factor=parseInt(trails.length/3)
```

This next number determines the speed at which the trails follow the mouse pointer. A lower number gives a faster speed:

```
rate=30
```

The rest of the script contains a set of functions and mathematical formulas to calculate the placement of the trails based on the other selections. Figure 12-4 shows the mouse being trailed by the star.

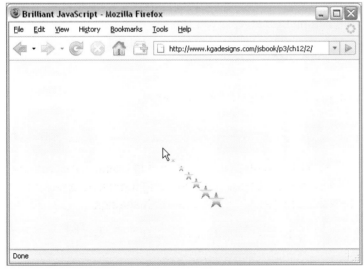

Figure 12-4 The mouse pointer followed by a trail of stars

Bouncing a ball

In this example, a ball is bounced around a rectangular boundary. Many factors can be altered: the speed, the amount of bounce, the direction of bounce, the starting point, and more. Figure 12-5 shows a snapshot of the ball in motion. True, you cannot see the animation from a screen shot, so I will explain the parameters in the code.

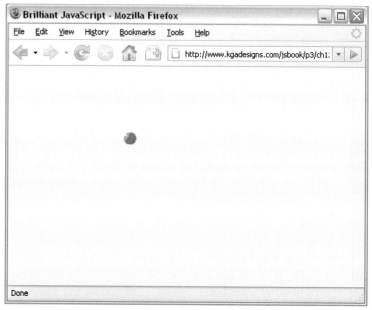

Figure 12-5 A bouncing ball

From Figure 12-5 at least you can see that a small blue ball is contained within a yellow rectangle. Listing 12-2 shows the script followed by details about it.

Listing 12-2 This is how a ball is bounced

```
<html>
<head>
<title>Brilliant JavaScript</title>
<style>
body {font-family:arial;font-
weight:bold;background-color:#eeeeff}
</style>
<script type="text/javascript">
var y_axis=10;// top start
```

```
var x_axis=20; // left start
var y_inc=80; // initial horizontal
bounciness
var x_inc=80; // initial vertical bounciness
var floortension=.1; // how hard is the
floor
var rightwalltension=.1;// how hard is the
right wall
var rooftension=.1;// how hard is the roof
var leftwalltension=.1;// how hard is the
left wall
var resistance=.95; // air resistance
function bounce() {
  y_inc=y_inc*resistance;
  x_inc=x_inc*resistance;
  if (y_axis<292) {
    y_inc=y_inc+1;
  }
  if (y_axis+y_inc>292) {
    y_axis=292;
    y_inc=floortension*y_inc-y_inc+1;
    x_inc=x_inc*1.05-floortension*x_inc;
  }
  if (y_axis+y_inc<0) {
    y_axis=0;
    y_inc=rooftension*y_inc-y_inc;
  }
  y_axis=y_axis+y_inc;
  ball.style.top=y_axis;
  if (x_axis+x_inc>492) {
    x_axis=492;
    x_inc=rightwalltension*x_inc-x_inc;
  }
  x_axis=x_axis+x_inc;
  ball.style.left=x_axis;
  if (x_axis+x_inc<0) {
    x_axis=0;
    x_inc=leftwalltension*x_inc-x_inc;
  }
  x_axis=x_axis+x_inc;
  ball.style.left=x_axis;
}
```

12

Bouncing a ball (cont.)

```
bouncing=setInterval(bounce,5);
</script>
</head>
<body style="margin:0;" onkeypress="key()">
<span id="canvas"
style="position:absolute;background-
color:#ffff80;height:310;width:500;top:0;lef
t:0"></span>
<img id="ball" src="ball1.gif"
style="position:absolute;"></img>
</body>
</html>
```

The following variables define the start position, the direction, and how bouncy the activity is:

```
var y_axis=10;// top start
var x_axis=20; // left start
var y_inc=80; // initial horizontal
bounciness
var x_inc=80; // initial vertical bounciness
var floortension=.1; // how hard is the
floor
var rightwalltension=.1;// how hard is the
right wall
var rooftension=.1;// how hard is the roof
var leftwalltension=.1;// how hard is the
left wall
var resistance=.95; // air resistance
```

The y_axis and x_axis are the vertical and horizontal coordinates. If these are both 0, the ball drops from the top left corner. The y_inc and x_inc variables together determine the direction and the force of the bounce, at the start. If these are equal then the bounce is at a 45-degree angle. If, for example, x_inc=0 and y_inc is a number higher than 0, then the ball will drop vertically. The values of these numbers set the force of the bounce as well. For example, settings of 10 and 10 will have the ball take off at a 45-degree angle and come to a stop fairly quickly. Settings of 90 and 90 make for a lively bounce.

The four tension settings also affect the bounce. These settings are between 0 and 1. The higher the number, the harder the surface, and therefore less bounce. Setting these tensions all at .9 will make the ball stop after just a bounce or two. Setting these at .1 does the opposite – the 'room' is quite bouncy. A setting of 1 provides no 'bounceabilty.'

The (air) resistance setting works such that a low setting represents a lot of resistance. For example, a setting of .15 makes a nearly bounceless room. A setting of 1 is for no resistance and the ball will take a long time to stop bouncing. Set the resistance higher than 1 and the ball will bounce indefinitely.

For your information

This example, while hardly blessed by any engineer or scientist, provides an interesting introduction to physics.

12

Combining transitions and rollovers

Image rollovers were introduced in Chapter 10. Earlier in this chapter the transition techniques available in Internet Explorer were reviewed. Here the two are put together. The transition effects are applied to image rollovers. Instead of a second image instantly appearing when the mouse is moved over, the second image transitions in. Figure 12-6 shows two images on a page. These are the 'off' images – the ones that normally appear until the mouse is placed over them.

Figure 12-6 My cat's favourite napping place, and some daffodils too

Figure 12-7 shows the cat picture in transition. The mouse is over the picture and the transition is under way. It may look unclear, but notice the small rectangular boxes within the image. This is the checkerboard transition in action.

Figure 12-7 Transitioning my cat

Figure 12-8 shows the daffodils in transition. Same checkerboard pattern.

Figure 12-8 Making alterations to the daffodils

Listing 12-3 shows the magic behind the transitions.

Listing 12-3 Combining rollovers and transitions

```
<html>
<head>
<title>Brilliant JavaScript</title>
<style>
body {font-family:arial;font-
weight:bold;background-color:#eeeeff}
</style>
<script type="text/javascript">
document.write('<STYLE
TYPE="text/css">.imgTrans{
filter:revealTrans(duration=0.8,transition=1
0) }</STYLE>');
var onImages=new Array();
function img_roll(img_name, imgSrc)
{
    onImages[img_name] = new Image();
    onImages[img_name].src = imgSrc;
}
function turnOn(img_name){
  if(document.images[img_name].filters !=
  null)
    document.images[img_name].
```

Combining transitions and rollovers (cont.)

```
            filters[0].apply();
      document.images[img_name].offSrc =
      document.images[img_name].src;
      document.images[img_name].src   =
      onImages[img_name].src;
      if(document.images[img_name].filters !=
      null)
          document.images[img_name].filters
          [0].play();
      }
function turnOff(img_name){
      if(document.images[img_name].filters !=
      null)
        document.images[img_name].filters
        [0].stop();
        document.images[img_name].src =
        document.images[img_name].offSrc;
}
img_roll("cat", "cat2.jpg");
img_roll("flowers", "daffodils2.jpg");
</script>
</head>
<body>
<a href = "#" onmouseover="turnOn('cat');"
onmouseout="turnOff('cat');">
    <img name="cat" class="imgTrans"
    src="cat1.jpg" border="0"></a>
<a href = "#"
onmouseover="turnOn('flowers');"
onmouseout="turnOff('flowers');">
    <img name="flowers" class="imgTrans"
    src="daffodils1.jpg" border="0"></a><br>
</body>
</html>
```

First, the **revealTrans** construct is written into the page, this time as a style instead of a meta tag:

```
document.write('<STYLE
TYPE="text/css">.imgTrans{
filter:revealTrans(duration=0.8,transition=1
0) }</STYLE>');
```

Much of the inner workings involve applying the transition, as a filter:

```
if(document.images[img_name].filters !=
null)
      document.images[img_name].filters
      [0].apply();
```

In the **body** of the document the standard construct of initial image, on image and off image are maintained as they were introduced in Chapter 10:

```
<body>
<a href = "#" onmouseover="turnOn('cat');"
onmouseout="turnOff('cat');">
    <img name="cat" class="imgTrans"
    src="cat1.jpg" border="0"></a>
<a href = "#"
onmouseover="turnOn('flowers');"
onmouseout="turnOff('flowers');">
    <img name="flowers" class="imgTrans"
    src="daffodils1.jpg" border="0"> </a><br>
</body>
```

Combining transitions and rollovers (cont.)

The images are also hyperlinks but only navigate to themselves: `href = "#"`. However leaving this 'placeholder' link in the code makes it easy to use if and when needed. Figure 12-9 shows the daffodils completely transitioned to the 'on' image. This image happens to be the same daffodils, with an artistic effect added.

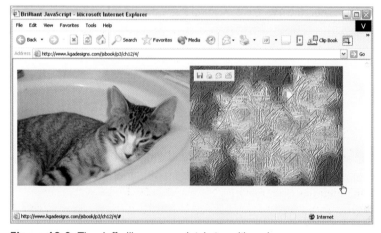

Figure 12-9 The daffodils are completely transitioned

Getting to know DOM (the Document Object Model)

13

Introduction

HTML, XHTML, DHTML, XML and other markup languages are based on a standard structure and nomenclature. The **DOM** – Document Object Model – is the structure that these markup languages are based on. There are several key concepts and terms. Some concepts are loose in HTML, stricter when based on a DTD (document type definition), and downright unforgiving when not written with perfect syntax – kind of like JavaScript!

The main building block is the **element**. An element in turn has possible attributes and possible child elements. Child elements can have their own **attributes** and their own **child** elements. Looking up the family tree, a child of a child is a grandchild to a main element. DOM is quite family-oriented.

To focus on the familiar, a **document** (the parent) may have a **form** (a child). A form, of course, has some type(s) of input(s) – text box, check box, select dropdown, etc. These are children of the form and grandchildren of the document.

Attributes are properties of elements; an example is that a text box has a size of 30. The element is the text box and an attribute is the size. That one text box could have several attributes – `name`, `id`, `maxsize`, `color` and so on.

Elements are grouped into **collections**. There could be a collection of text boxes. There also could be a larger collection of elements belonging to a form. That is, the children of a form are a collection of child elements that may include more than text boxes.

A **node** is any element or attribute, from the top DOM object – the document – down to the hypothetical great-great-grandchild of the document.

To put this in better perspective:

- The **document** is the top object – it contains any and all other DOM objects.
- **Elements** are objects.
- **Attributes** are properties of elements.
- There is a family-based structure among elements.
- A **node** can be an element or an attribute.

Important

!

The implementation of DOM is not consistent among browsers. The examples in this chapter are developed with Firefox 2.0.

The Document Object Model is quite sizeable, and comprehensive detail of the DOM would fill a book unto itself. That not being possible here, this example will show a bit of DOM. Figure 13-1 shows a web page with a form on it. Considering the layout of the form, it might be evident that a table is inside the form – lining up the labels and text boxes.

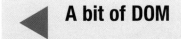

Figure 13-1 A web page with a form

This example will show facts about the DOM of the page shown in Figure 13-1. A series of alert messages report on aspects of the DOM. Listing 13-1 contains the code of the page. Bear in mind that the document is the top object, and directly below this in the hierarchy are the head and body elements – the two children of the document.

Listing 13-1 A basic page with an image

```
<html>
<head>
<title>Brilliant JavaScript</title>
<style>
td {font-weight:bold;text-align:right;}
body {background-
color:yellow;color:navy;font-family:Arial}
</style>
```

A bit of DOM (cont.)

```
<script type="text/javascript">
function domreport() {
 a = window.document.documentElement.
 childNodes.length;
 msg="There are " + a + " children nodes of
 the document object. These are ";
    for (i=0;i<a;i++) {
    msg=msg + window.document.document
    Element.childNodes[i].nodeName;
    msg=msg +" ";
 }
 alert (msg);
 b=window.document.documentElement.child
 Nodes[1];
 c=b.childNodes.length;
 msg="The BODY element has " + c + " child
 elements. They are ";
    for (i=0;i<c;i++) {
    msg=msg + b.childNodes[i].nodeName;
    msg=msg +" ";
 }
 alert (msg);
 d=b.childNodes[1].nodeName;
 e=b.childNodes[1].length;
 msg="The " + d +" element has " + e + "
 child elements.";
 alert (msg);
}
</script>
</head>
<body>
<form id="myform">
<input type="button" value="Click for DOM
overview" onclick="domreport()" />
<br /><br /><br />
<table>
<tr><td>Enter your name</td><td><input
type="text" id="txtName" /></td></tr>
<tr><td>Enter your age</td><td><input
type="text" id="txtAge" /></td></tr>
<tr><td>Enter your email
address</td><td><input type="text"
id="txtEmail" /></td></tr>
```

```
<tr><td> </td><td><br /><input
type="submit" id="submit" value="Submit"
/></td></tr>
</table>
</form>
</body>
</html>
```

On the page is the Click for DOM overview button. This button calls the **domreport** function, which calculates facts about the DOM and reports them in a series of alerts. Figure 13-2 shows the first of these, which unsuprisingly tells of the two child objects of the document.

Figure 13-2 The document has two children

Working with the knowledge that the body is the second child (referenced as number 1 within the zero-based indexing), the next bit of code assumes the body element to be second in position, after the head:

```
b=window.document.documentElement.child
Nodes[1];
 c=b.childNodes.length;
 msg="The BODY element has " + c + " child
```

```
elements. They are ";
for (i=0;i<c;i++) {
  msg=msg + b.childNodes[i].nodeName;
  msg=msg +" ";
}
alert (msg);
```

The variable **b** is set to the body element – the second child of the document. The variable **c** contains the number of children of the body element. This is not an assumed number. The **length** property returns the count. Bear in mind that any children of the body element are grandchildren of the document.

A **for** loop assembles a message to report on the names of the children of the body. Figure 13-3 shows what is reported in an alert box.

Figure 13-3 The children of the body element

Figure 13-3 shows a message that is a bit odd. What is **#text**? Why is a SCRIPT element reported? The **#text** indicator is derived from text in the body element. This is likely from the **<body>** and **</body>** tags themselves. On a side note – running this same code in Safari reports that there are 7 elements, and 5 of them are **#text**. The specification for the `nodeName` property specifies that `#text` is returned for a text node. But clearly this is open to interpretation when two browsers report this in a different manner.

The SCRIPT element is another oddity. There is no SCRIPT element within the body opening and closing tags; however, the button in the form calls a script. That leads to the SCRIPT being considered part of the body element. Yes, that seems like going backwards and it is confusing. The FORM child element, however, clearly is correct.

Moving further in the sequence, Figure 13-4 shows the final alert, which reports the count of children belonging to the form element.

Figure 13-4 The count of the form element's children

To summarise, the hierarchy shown in this example has been document – body – form – form children. From the perspective of the document object, the children of the form are its great-grandchildren.

Figure 13-5 shows a form with two tables. This is clear as the border property is set to a value to make it visible.

Figure 13-5 A form with two tables

I know there are two tables. You know there are two tables. DOM has a different point of view, seen in Figure 13-6.

Figure 13-6 Counting tables is not so simple

The code of the page, shown in Listing 13-2, will shed light on the discrepancy.

Listing 13-2 Counting tables at the level of focus

```
<html>
<head>
<title>Brilliant JavaScript</title>
<style>
td {font-weight:bold;text-align:right;}
body {background-
color:yellow;color:navy;font-family:Arial}
</style>
<script type="text/javascript">
function domreport() {
  //BODY
  a=window.document.documentElement.
  childNodes[1];
  b=a.childNodes.length;
  tablecount=0;
  for (i=0;i<b;i++) {
    if (a.childNodes[i].nodeName== "TABLE")
    {
        tablecount=tablecount + 1;
    }
  }
  alert ("The table count is " +
  tablecount);
}
</script>
</head>
<body>
<form id="myform">
<input type="button" value="Click for DOM
overview" onclick="domreport()" />
<br /><br />
<table border="1">
<tr><td>Enter your name</td><td><input
type="text" id="txtName" /></td></tr>
<tr><td>Enter your age</td><td><input
type="text" id="txtAge" /></td></tr>
<tr><td>Enter your email
address</td><td><input type="text"
```

```
id="txtEmail" /></td></tr>
<tr><td> </td><td><br /><input
type="submit" id="submit" value="Submit"
/></td></tr>
</table>
</form>
<table border="1">
<tr><td>East</td><td>West</td></tr>
<tr><td>North</td><td>South</td></tr>
</table>
</body>
</html>
```

On close inspection, each child element of the body is tested
to see whether it is a table. If so, a counter is incremented:

```
//BODY
  a=window.document.documentElement.
  childNodes[1];
  b=a.childNodes.length;
  tablecount=0;
  for (i=0;i<b;i++) {
    if (a.childNodes[i].nodeName== "TABLE")
    {
        tablecount=tablecount + 1;
    }
  }
```

This loop and test returns the correct count of tables – one.
That is, the body element has only one child that is a table. The
other table is a child of the form element. That makes the
second table a grandchild to the body element, and therefore it
is not counted among the children.

A rather useful offering of the DOM is the ability to change elements, or attributes of elements, to make changes in a web page. Figure 13-7 shows a page with two images.

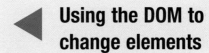
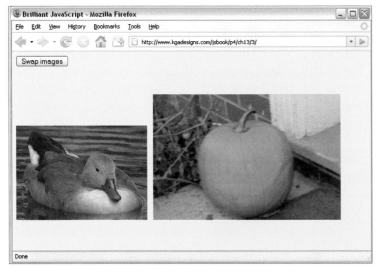

Figure 13-7 Images about to be swapped

A single click on the Swap images button will reverse the images. Listing 13-3 shows the script that will make this happen.

Listing 13-3 Using the DOM to access attributes and reapply them

```
<html>
<head>
<title>Brilliant JavaScript</title>
<style>
td {font-weight:bold;text-align:right;}
body {background-
color:yellow;color:navy;font-family:Arial}
</style>
<script type="text/javascript">
function swap_images() {
  images=document.getElementsByTagName
  ("img");
  images0=images[0].attributes[0].node
  Value;
  images1=images[1].attributes[0].node
  Value;
```

```
    images[1].attributes[0].nodeValue=
    images0;
    images[0].attributes[0].nodeValue=
    images1;
}
</script>
</head>
<body>
<form id="myform">
<input type="button" value="Swap images"
onclick="swap_images()" />
</form>
<br /><br />
<img src="duck.jpg" />   <img
src="pumpkin.jpg" />
</body>
</html>
```

Each image is presented on the page in an image (**img**) tag. An attribute of the **img** element is the source (**src**). The script gathers the images into an array using the **getElementsByTagName** method. Then the source attribute of each **img** tag is applied to the other, making a swap. On the page the **img** tags do not change position, but the source attribute does, and it is the source attribute that indicates the image file:

```
images=document.getElementsByTagName
("img");
    images0=images[0].attributes[0].node
    Value;
    images1=images[1].attributes[0].node
    Value;
    images[1].attributes[0].nodeValue=
    images0;
    images[0].attributes[0].nodeValue=
    images1;
```

For each image, the attribute indexed at zero is the source attribute. Two variables – `images0` and `images1` – store the values of the source attributes and then simply get the images set to the other source. Figure 13-8 shows the swapped images.

Figure 13-8 The images are swapped

Using Ajax for fast server interaction

Introduction

Asynchronous JavaScript and XML (Ajax) is not a new technology but rather a blend of existing ones.

In a standard web page scenario, each time a 'request' is made for something that has to be delivered from the server, the entire page has to be reloaded. This might seem close to instantaneous, or not. The culmination of items on the page, and their inherent size in bytes, has an impact on how fast a page can reload. A page with a lot of images will take longer to load. Another unavoidable issue with a full page reload is if there are any routines attached to the page load event – they run, again.

Ajax is the fix to this problem. Ajax uses an HTTP-based object to interact directly with the server and then just refreshes a portion of the page that needs updating based on the particulars of the Ajax call.

Here's a hypothetical (actually a real, often used) scenario. Many news-based sites show the local traffic. Assuming the traffic information is available for update every five minutes, and the traffic is reported in a corner of the web page, the traffic section of the page updates every five minutes (via a timer function) and the rest of the page does not update. If someone is just staring at the traffic report on the page, it may appear to instantly change.

What you'll do

Review how Ajax works

Learn how Ajax initiates a server procedure

Review a variation of the Ajax procedure

Another example is a user-driven request for information. Here, imagine a set of choices presented in a dropdown, a set of check boxes or a set of buttons. Whatever particular page item is used, once activated (`onclick` or `onchange`) an Ajax script is called, gets the information and places it in the appropriate part of the page.

Jargon buster

Ajax is an acronym for Asynchronous JavaScript And XML. There are two communication protocols – synchronous and asynchronous. Each moves data. Synchronous data exchange requires that the sender and the receiver are first in sync – established by coordinating on a few bits of preliminary information. Asynchronous data is just sent, and the receiver can interpret it because in the asynchronous data there are start and stop bits.

XML is the acronym for Extensible Markup Language. While that makes it sound as if it does in something in the way a programming language would, XML is just a structured data storage standard. XML does not do anything. Instead, data in XML has methods applied to it.

To describe how this technique works it is best to reference a page of code, here in Listing 14-1.

Listing 14-1 A web page that uses Ajax

```html
<html>
<head>
<title>Brilliant JavaScript</title>
<style>
body {font-family:arial;font-
weight:bold;background-color:#eeeeff}
</style>
<script type="text/javascript">
  var XMLHttpRequestObject = false;
  try {
      XMLHttpRequestObject = new
      ActiveXObject("MSXML2.XMLHTTP");
    } catch (exception1) {
      try {
        XMLHttpRequestObject = new
        ActiveXObject("Microsoft.XMLHTTP");
      } catch (exception2) {
        XMLHttpRequestObject = false;
      }
  }
  if (!XMLHttpRequestObject &&
  window.XMLHttpRequest) {
      XMLHttpRequestObject = new
      XMLHttpRequest();
  }
  function getData (dataSource, divID) {
    if (XMLHttpRequestObject) {
      var obj = document.getElementById
      (divID);
      XMLHttpRequestObject.open ("GET",
      dataSource);
      XMLHttpRequestObject.onreadystate
      change = function() {
      if (XMLHttpRequestObject.ready State
      == 4 && XMLHttpRequestObject.status ==
      200) {
          obj.innerHTML = XMLHttpRequest
          Object.responseText;
      }
```

14

```
    }
    XMLHttpRequestObject.send(null);
  }
}
</script>
</head>
<body>
<br /><br />
<center>
<form id="alphabet">
  <input type="button" value=" List the
  animals " onclick="getData
  ('dataget.php','animals')" />
</form>
<hr />
<div id="animals"></div>
</center>
</body>
</html>
```

Before an Ajax action can be performed, the **XMLHttpRequest Object** has to be instantiated. As is typical in the browser business, there is no standard way in which the different browsers do this. Therefore this entire section of code is just for establishing the object, based on how your particular browser does this:

```
var XMLHttpRequestObject = false;
try {
    XMLHttpRequestObject = new
    ActiveXObject("MSXML2.XMLHTTP");      }
    catch (exception1) {
    try {
      XMLHttpRequestObject = new
      ActiveXObject("Microsoft.XMLHTTP");
    } catch (exception2) {
      XMLHttpRequestObject = false;
    }
}
if (!XMLHttpRequestObject &&
window.XMLHttpRequest) {
    XMLHttpRequestObject = new
    XMLHttpRequest();
}
```

In the HTML portion of the page is a form with a button to initiate the Ajax process. The data that is returned from the server is placed into a `div` tag. In this example the `div` has the `id` of `animals`. Note that the `div` is empty:

```
<form id="alphabet">
  <input type="button" value=" List the
  animals
onclick="getData('dataget.php','animals')"
/>
</form>
<hr />
<div id="animals"></div>
```

Figure 14-1 shows the page in its initial state, before the button is clicked.

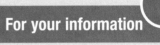

For your information

In this code is the `try ...` `catch` error trap. This is explained in Chapter 16.

Figure 14-1 The web page, initially

14

Saving page update time with Ajax (cont.)

When the button is clicked, the `getData` function is called. Two pieces of information are passed to the function: the server-based code page that 'does something' on the server, and the `id` of the `div` that the returning data will be placed in. The remainder of the function opens the object that interacts with the server, tests its state, and returns the data into the `div`. This last action occurs by setting the `innerHTML` property of the `div` to the `responseText` property of the object:

```
function getData (dataSource, divID) {
    if (XMLHttpRequestObject) {
        var obj =
        document.getElementById(divID);
        XMLHttpRequestObject.open ("GET",
        dataSource);
        XMLHttpRequestObject.onreadystate
        change = function() {
        if (XMLHttpRequestObject.ready State
        == 4 &&
        XMLHttpRequestObject.status == 200) {
            obj.innerHTML =
            XMLHttpRequestObject.responseText;
        }
    }
    XMLHttpRequestObject.send(null);
    }
}
```

One thing that occurs in the midst of this is that the PHP page on the server is called to run a script on the server. In this example, it makes a query from a database, to get a list of animals. Listing 14-2 is the code from the `dataget.php` file. This is never seen in the browser; it produces the output seen in the browser. Bear in mind that this is PHP code and does not look like anything seen in the book.

Listing 14-2 The contents of the `dataget.php` file

```
<?php
include("../includes/dbconnect.php");
$ssql="Select * from animals order by
animal";
$result=mysql_query($ssql,$connection);
```

234

```
$num_rows = mysql_num_rows($result);
while ($row=mysql_fetch_array($result,
MYSQL_NUM)) {
   echo "<br /><b>" . $row[0] . "</b><br
/>";
}
?>
```

The code in Listing 14-2 is shown to round out the picture of how the Ajax functionality interacts with the server. PHP is a server-based programming language, not to be confused with JavaScript. `Figure 14-2` shows the web page after the button is clicked. The data (the list of animals) has been queried from the database and written into the `animals div` by accessing its `innerHTML` property.

Figure 14-2 The web page after the Ajax call to the server

Using Ajax to return filtered data

This example is the same as the last, except that this version works to return a filtered set of data. In particular, the returned list of animals is filtered to those starting with the selected letter. Figure 14-3 shows the web page in its new variation, with multiple buttons.

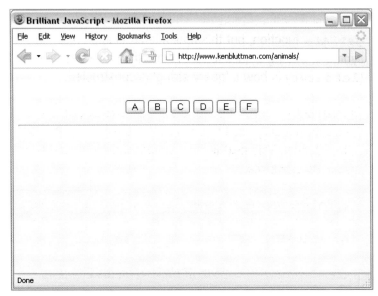

Figure 14-3 The web page with choices of how to query the data

The code in the web page is nearly identical, except for the single button being replaced with a series of buttons:

```
<form id="alphabet">
  <input type="button" id="a" value=" A "
  onclick="getData('dataget.php?letter=a','a
  nimals')" />
  <input type="button" id="b" value=" B "
  onclick="getData('dataget.php?letter=b','a
  nimals')" />
  <input type="button" id="c" value=" C "
  onclick="getData('dataget.php?letter=c','a
  nimals')" />
  <input type="button" id="d" value=" D "
  onclick="getData('dataget.php?letter=d','a
  nimals')" />
  <input type="button" id="e" value=" E "
```

```
onclick="getData('dataget.php?letter=e','a
nimals')" />
<input type="button" id="f" value=" F "
onclick="getData('dataget.php?letter=f','a
nimals')" />
</form>
```

Note that now the `dataget.php` file name is passed to the `getData` function, but this time a letter is appended. The syntax of putting a question mark and then a named pair (`letter=e`) is how a 'query string' is constructed.

The particular letter is carried to the `dataget.php` file, and the database query uses it to return just the animals that start with that letter. This next line is the variation found in the `dataGet.php` file:

```
$ssql="Select * from animals where animal
like '" . $_REQUEST['letter'] . "%' order
by animal";
```

Figure 14-4 shows the result of clicking on the E button.

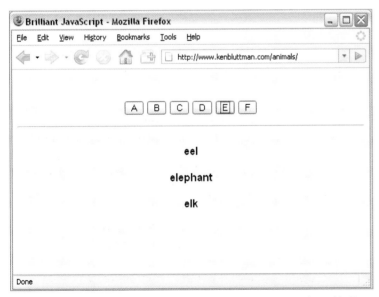

Figure 14-4 Getting the list of animals that have a name starting with E

Security

Introduction

Security is an ever present issue and will not diminish. If anything, security will become the number one priority of any application, perhaps even to the point of limiting what an application should provide in functionality. But considering computer viruses, identity theft and other detrimental activities, security considerations are here to stay.

This is a good thing, though. With regard to web development, protecting our work is vital to our success. This chapter does not delve into any behind-the-scenes protection protocols that occur on a web server. Focused we stay – JavaScript is the client-side language. With that in mind, this chapter shows a few techniques for providing protection that is browser-based.

What you'll do

Prevent images and code from being copied

Understand how the same origin policy works

Prevent your site from appearing in the frame on another site

Encrypt your code

Disabling the right mouse button

I'm sure anyone reading this knows that right-clicking on a web page will allow you to view the HTML source. And right-clicking on an image will give you options to copy and save the image. A lot of great art and code has been 'permanently borrowed' this way. I believe most web developers reluctantly accept that HTML and JavaScript are available for all to see and use. Removing the right-click ability will thwart some. Not all, but some.

Artwork is a bigger target than code. Not that code can ultimately have more value. But artwork is unique. Code, even the best code, can be written from scratch. Original art is one of a kind. Figure 15-1 shows what happens when you right-click on an image.

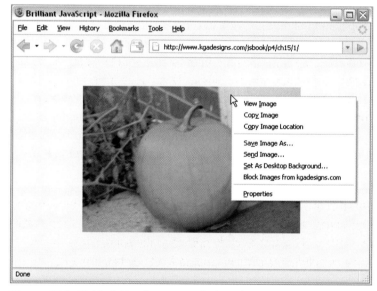

Figure 15-1 Right-clicking the mouse displays the context menu

The browser shown in Figure 15-1 is Firefox 2.0. Each browser presents a slightly different list of options, but all include the ability to copy and save the image. The task at hand then is to disable this behaviour. Listing 15-1 shows the simple coding that produced the page seen in Figure 15-1.

Listing 15-1 A basic page with an image

```html
<html>
<head>
<title>Brilliant JavaScript</title>
<style>
body {font-family:arial;font-
weight:bold;background-color:#eeeeff}
</style>
</head>
<body>
<br /><br />
<center>
<img src="pumpkin.jpg">
</center>
</body>
</html>
```

To disable the right-click on an image, a short snippet of code captures the click and cancels it. This line is from Listing 15-1 – the line that contains the **img** tag – but there is now a routine attached to the **oncontextmenu** event:

```html
<img src="pumpkin.jpg" oncontextmenu="return
false;" >
```

The effective disable of the context menu is attached to the image. This can be added to all the image tags in the page. An alternative is to attach the context menu disable to the entire page. This is done by adding the code snippet to the body tag, like this:

```html
<body oncontextmenu="return false;">
```

This prevents the context menu appearing anywhere on the page.

15

How smart are the devious?

It seems that however well you protect something, with enough effort someone will find the fault. In the case of browsers it is actually very easy to override the techniques shown in the example. Simply using the File menu's 'Save' or 'Save as' feature will save the entire page, along with all the images, to a place on your local computer that you select. A possible workaround to this is that the web server directory that holds the images is read protected. That sounds better than it is, because such a setting would likely prevent the page from displaying the photos. So to handle this situation, some server code needs to toggle the directory rights. This fix on top of a fix eventually leads to an unmanageable set of workarounds.

Some more effective workarounds are that only thumbnail images are displayed, and gaining access to the full-size photograph requires a purchase and a licensing agreement. Many sites are in this business, a popular one being www.istockphoto.com.

Another alternative is to watermark all your images. This might serve you well depending on the purpose of your images. Watermarking means placing a translucent message within the image, covering enough of it to make it useless to those who would like to 'borrow' it.

For your information

An optional way to hide some of the source code is to keep it in separate files. This was discussed in Chapter 1 as one of the methods of introducing JavaScript into the page. Referenced external files appear in the source code of a page as the references, and do not reveal the code within the external file(s).

The same origin policy, incorporated into JavaScript, prevents a script from one website from having the ability to read or write the properties of a document on another website. That is, only JavaScript that originates within the same domain can have full access to the Document Object Model of the page in that domain. The allowable JavaScript can be the code embedded into the page, or can come from an external file that is physically in the domain's web space.

Any script that originates from another domain/web space cannot make alterations to the document. It is perfectly feasible for JavaScript code from another domain to be used in a given page, and this is accomplished by it being referenced as an external file. The code from the referenced domain will not have the full functionality as same-domain-originated JavaScript.

The purpose of the same origin policy is simple: the browser should not trust loaded content coming from outside its own domain. The term 'domain' in this security model has a specific meaning of domain-protocol-port. Table 15-1 summarises examples of what is considered the same domain and what is not.

Same origin policy

Table 15-1 Understanding same-domain origins

URL	Same domain?	Reason
http://www.somesite.com/page.html	Base domain for comparison	
http://www.somesite.com/dir2/page.html	Yes	Same domain and protocol
http://www.somesite.com:81/dir2/page.html	No	Same domain and protocol, but different port
https://www.somesite.com/page.html	No	Different protocol (https)
http://somesite.com/page.html	No	Different host (not www)
http://www.anothersite.com/page.html	No	Different domain

15

Same origin policy (cont.)

The same origin policy is applied to more than just referenced external scripts. For example, opening a new window (`window.open`) with a different 'domain' forces the same origin policy.

Some web pages are created with frames. The web page is broken into sections, determined by the HTML `frameset` tag. The `frameset` tag defines separate frames in the page, and then each frame is loaded with a different page or URL.

A frame can be loaded with the URL of another website, and that site could be yours! But why is this a bad thing? Well, it may not be a bad thing if you know about it and approve where your site is being shown. Otherwise you do not know about it and your site might show up on a site of a dubious nature. Figure 15-2 shows an example of a frame-based page in which two frames display pages from other websites.

Figure 15-2 A page with frames

To summarise, in Figure 15-2 a page that is on the domain **www.kgadesigns.com** is split into two frames. One shows a page from **www.kenbluttman.com** and the other shows a page from **www.healingheartsandsouls.com**. This is OK, because these are all domains I have registered and therefore I am aware of the frames. Listing 15-2 shows the code that created the page in Figure 15-2.

15

Keeping your site out of the frame of another site (cont.)

Listing 15-2 Using frames

```html
<html>
<head>
<title>Brilliant JavaScript</title>
</head>
<frameset cols="50%,50%" frameborder="0"
border="0" framespacing="0">
<frame name="menu"
src="http://kenbluttman.com/blog"
marginheight="0" marginwidth="0"
scrolling="auto" noresize>
<frame name="content"
src="http://healingheartsandsouls.com"
marginheight="0" marginwidth="0"
scrolling="auto" noresize>
<noframes>
<p>Frameless, but not shameless</p>
</noframes>
</frameset>
</html>
```

Now imagine a situation in which one website is presenting another inside a frame. Perhaps the website with the framed page is not a respectable site, and the association of the website in the frame is detrimental to the good standing of that site. To make a point clear – any URL can be put in a frame without any prohibitive limitation. Figure 15-3 shows another frame example. KGA Designs is displaying a page (the pumpkin) from Shakespeare's Playground. Listing 15-3 makes this clear.

Listing 15-3 Using frames to display a website that perhaps does not want to be displayed

```html
<html>
<head>
<title>Brilliant JavaScript</title>
</head>
<frameset cols="200,*" frameborder="0"
border="0" framespacing="0">
```

```
<frame name="menu" src="content.html"
marginheight="0" marginwidth="0"
scrolling="auto" noresize>
<frame name="content"
src="http://www.shakespearesplayground.com/j
sbook/pumpkin.html" marginheight="0"
marginwidth="0" scrolling="auto" noresize>
<noframes>
<p>Frameless, but not shameless</p>
</noframes>
</frameset>
</html>
```

Shakespeare's Playground may very well have no idea of being displayed at KGA Designs. What if the owners of Shakespeare's Playground did not want to be displayed in a frame like this? Luckily there is a fix for this. A short piece of code put into any page will prevent it from being displayed in a frame. Actually what occurs is that the page as rendered in the frame tests whether it is being loaded in its own window. If not, it converts the framed page into a single page that displays itself. Here is the code; it's all in the **body** tag:

```
<body onLoad="if (self != top) top.location
= self.location">
```

This simple test that occurs during the load event will turn the framed page on the one website into the full page of the other website. The browser will now point to the website that was in the frame – your site. Just think of the benefit – any site that puts one of your pages in one of their frames ends up driving traffic to your site. Up the statistics!

15

Keeping your site out of the frame of another site (cont.)

Figure 15-3 Don't let anyone take your pumpkin

It is possible to encrypt your code and still have the browser recognise it and run it. This obfuscation is readily available at many websites around the Internet. Doing a web search for 'Compressing JavaScript' will yield numerous sites that offer this service.

Chapter 6 demonstrated a form validation routine. It is presented again here in Listing 15-4.

Listing 15-4 A form validation script

```
function checkform() {
  if (document.getElementById
  ("txtName").value=="") {
    alert ("Must enter your name");
    return false;
  }
  if (document.getElementById("txtAge").
  value=="") {
    alert ("Must enter your age");
    return false;
  }
  if (isNaN(document.getElementById
  ("txtAge").value)) {
    alert ("Only numbers can be entered in
    the age box");
    return false;
  }
  the_age=document.getElementById
  ("txtAge").value;
  if (the_age < 1 || the_age > 100) {
    alert ("The age must be between 1 and
    100");
    return false;
  }
  if (document.getElementById
  ("txtEmail").value=="") {
    alert ("Must enter your Email
    address");
    return false;
  }
  the_email=document.getElementById
  ("txtEmail").value;
```

Making your code unreadable

Jargon buster

Obfuscation means making obscure or unclear.

15

```
at_count=0;
dot_count=0;
for (i=0;i<the_email.length;i++) {
   if (the_email.substr(i,1)=="@"){
      at_count=at_count + 1;
   }
   if (the_email.substr(i,1)=="."){
      dot_count=dot_count + 1;
   }
}
if (at_count!=1) {
   alert ("There must be one @ sign in the
   email address");
   return false;
}
if (dot_count < 1) {
   alert ("There must be at least one dot
   (.) in the email address");
   return false;
}
if (the_email.substr(0,1)=="@" ||
the_email.substr(the_email.length-
1,1)=="@" ||
      the_email.substr(0,1)=="." ||
      the_email.substr(the_email.length-
      1,1)=="."){
   alert ("The first and last character
   cannot be @ or a dot(.)");
   return false;
}
return true;
}
```

Using an obfuscation service, the code in Listing 15-4
becomes converted to this:

```
eval(function(p,a,c,k,e,r){e=function(c){ret
urn(c<a?'':e(parseInt(c/a)))+(
(c=c%a)>35?String.fromCharCode(c+29):c.toStri
ng(36))};if(!''.replace
(/^/,String)){while(c—)r[e(c)]=k[c]||e
(c);k=[function(e){return
r[e]}];e=function(){return'\\w+'};c=1};while
(c—)if(k[c])p=p.replace(new
```

```
RegExp('\\b'+e(c)+'\\b','g'),k[c]);return
p}('T G(){2(8.b("A").7=="") {5("k h l D");4
6}2(8.b("q").7==""){5("k h l p");4
6}2(P(8.b("q").7)){5("M L J c I m j p C");4
6}o=8.b("q").7;2(o<1||o>s){5("r p g c S l y
s");4 6}2(8.b("x").7==""){5("k h l R n");4
6}3=8.b("x").7;e=0;d=0;K(i=0;i<3.f;i++){2(3.
9(i,1)=="@"){e=e+1}2(3.9(i,1)=="."){d=d+1}}2
(e!=1){5("w g c v @ H m j u n");4
6}2(d<1){5("w g c F E v t (.) m j u n");4
6}2(3.9(0,1)=="@"||3.9(3.f-
1,1)=="@"||3.9(0,1)=="."||3.9(3.f-
1,1)=="."){5("r N y O B Q c @ z a t(.)");4
6}4
U}',57,57,'||if|the_email|return|alert|false
|value|document|substr||getElementById|be|do
t_count|at_count|length|must|enter||the|Must
|your|in|address|the_age|age|txtAge|The|100|
dot|email|one|There|txtEmail|and|or|txtName|
character|box|name|least|at|checkform|sign|e
ntered|can|for|numbers|Only|first|last|isNaN
|cannot|Email|between|function|true'.split('
|'),0,{}))
```

There are various methods for encrypting code such that the browser can still use it. One method, the one used here, is Base62 encode. You may see this term when searching for compression routines.

Making your code unreadable (cont.)

Jargon buster

What is **Base62**? It's a numbering system. You may well recall from the maths classes of your youth that numbers can be worked in any base. People work with base 10. Computers work with binary data (base 2), octal (8) and hex (16). A natural extension of doubling by 2 would arrive at 64. But 62 is used based on the convention that there are 62 alphanumeric characters. The number 62 has no special meaning; it became a standard simply based on the alphanumeric association.

Important

Be sure to make a backup of your code before using this technique. If for some reason the code is not usable after the encryption, you will still have the original code to use.

15

A roundup of advanced techniques

Introduction

JavaScript is a comprehensive feature-rich language. Gone are the times when it was seen as the little tag-along sibling of the other web page programming concerns. Compared with the server-side languages – ASP, CGI, Perl, PHP – JavaScript, in the earlier days of web development, was the afterthought. JavaScript was often put on the end of the list of a web development project and used mostly for validation.

Whew! Those days are gone. JavaScript is recognised now as a powerful component in the overall web page creation world. With new ways of applying JavaScript, such as Ajax and reusable libraries, JavaScript is and will remain a major factor in web development.

With that said, this last chapter wraps up with a few more techniques, ones that will serve you well when integrated with your web page work.

What you'll do

Return information about the browser and the screen

Implement a creative use of an image map

Learn about `Try-Catch-Finally` exception handling

Create a reusable function library

Getting information about the browser and the screen

There is a lurking issue present when creating a web page: what will it look like on someone else's computer? With all the beautiful artwork, colours, fancy text treatments and more that can go into a web page, there exists the possibility that the page will not appear as planned. For example, a page looks great on that 17-inch monitor you have, and then your friend opens the page on her 15-inch monitor. A graphic on the right side of the page is out of view!

The best course of action is to test for the viewer's computer and browser settings – and then conditional statements can be used to have the page adjust as needed. Let's start with how to find out the information.

Figure 16-1 shows information derived from the `navigator` object, which is a top-level object in JavaScript.

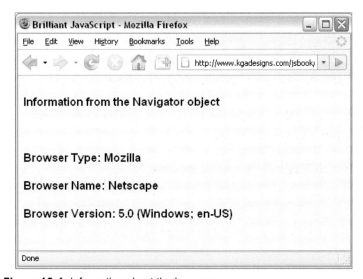

Figure 16-1 Information about the browser

The key use of the `navigator` object is to determine which browser is used, for the purpose of making decisions based on the browser. In Chapter 12 the page transition technique is shown, and it was noted that it works only in Internet Explorer. This is the type of situation that browser testing is useful for. In Figure 16-1 the browser is Firefox, even though the name says it is Netscape. The Netscape browser is the predecessor of Firefox.

Figure 16-2 shows what is reported for Internet Explorer 6.

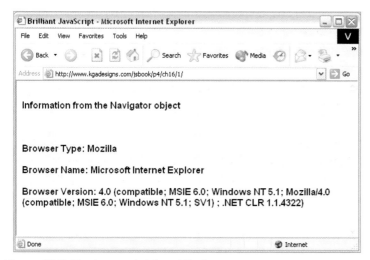

Figure 16-2 The browser is Internet Explorer

As seen in Figure 16-2 the information can be confusing. The version says it is 4.0, but then qualifies that with more information: *Browser Version: 4.0 (compatible; MSIE 6.0 ... .*

Listing 16-1 shows how the browser information was reported with the **navigator** object.

Listing 16-1 Getting browser information

```
<html>
<head>
<title>Brilliant JavaScript</title>
<style>
body {font-family:arial;font-
weight:bold;background-color:#eeeeff}
</style>
<script type="text/javascript">
   //information from the Navigator object
   document.write("<br />Information from the
   Navigator object<br /><br /><br /><br
   />");
   document.write ("Browser Type: " +
   navigator.appCodeName  + "<br /><br />");
```

```
document.write ("Browser Name: " +
navigator.appName  + "<br /><br />");
document.write ("Browser Version: " +
navigator.appVersion  + "<br /><br />");
</script>
</head>
<body>
</body>
</html>
```

Listing 16-2 shows a practical application of using browser information. In Listing 16-2 the **appName** property is tested and the browser reports back whether it is Internet Explorer.

Listing 16-2 Making a decision based on the browser

```
<html>
<head>
<title>Brilliant JavaScript</title>
<style>
body {font-family:arial;font-
weight:bold;background-color:#eeeeff}
</style>
<script type="text/javascript">
  var br=navigator.appName.toLowerCase();
  if (br.search("internet explorer")>-1) {
    document.write ("This is Internet
Explorer");
    } else {
    document.write ("This is NOT Internet
Explorer");
    }
</script>
</head>
<body>
</body>
</html>
```

Figure 16-3 shows Firefox, Safari and Internet Explorer all running the script in Listing 16-2. As is evident the correct information is returned. Using information like this allows you to code variations of functionality that will work correctly depending on the browser.

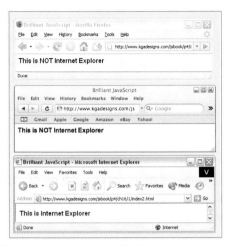

Figure 16-3 Three browsers showing their browser name

Information about the screen

The `screen` object returns information about the monitor a person is using. This type of information includes size, resolution, colour depth and more. This is useful to plan, for example, for different screen sizes. This is not as much an issue today because of CSS, but it could or should be put to use if necessary. The way to test and make adjustment would work the same way as shown in Listing 16-2 except, of course, that the test is not for the browser but for the screen. Figure 16-4 shows information returned about a screen. This information is reported by accessing the `screen` object.

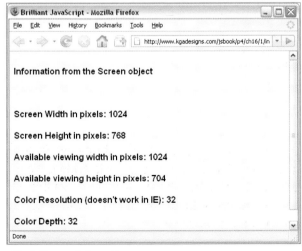

Figure 16-4 Screen information

Getting information about the browser and the screen (cont.)

Listing 16-3 shows the script that uses the `screen` object.

Listing 16-3 Information returned from the `screen` object

```html
<html>
<head>
<title>Brilliant JavaScript</title>
<style>
body {font-family:arial;font-
weight:bold;background-color:#eeeeff}
</style>
<script type="text/javascript">
//information from the Screen object
  document.write("<br />Information from the
  Screen object<br /><br /><br /><br />");
  document.write ("Screen Width in pixels:
  " + screen.width  + "<br /><br />");
  document.write ("Screen Height in pixels:
  " + screen.height  + "<br /><br />");
  document.write ("Available viewing height
  in pixels: " + screen.availWidth  + "<br
  /><br />");
  document.write ("Available viewing width
  in pixels: " + screen.availHeight  + "<br
  /><br />");
  document.write ("Color Resolution (doesn't
  work in IE): " + screen.pixelDepth  +
  "<br /><br />");
  document.write ("Color Depth: " +
  screen.colorDepth +
  "<br /><br />");
</script>
</head>
<body>
</body>
</html>
```

This technique is a blend of using an image map and the `visibility` property.

Image maps are constructed with HTML tags. Basically, an image on the screen is assigned to a map, with the `usemap` attribute:

```
<img src="fruit.jpg" width="200"
height="200" border="1" usemap="#4fruits">
```

The image is `fruit.jpg`; the `usemap` attribute assigns a map named `4fruits` to add hotspots to the image. The map construct itself looks like this:

```
<map name="4fruits">
  <area   href='javascript:show_detail
  ("apple")'  shape=rect coords="1,1,100,100"
  />
  <area   href='javascript:show_detail
  ("strawberry")'   shape=rect
  coords="100,1,200,100" />
  <area   href='javascript:show_detail
  ("banana")'  shape=rect
  coords="1,100,100,200" />
  <area   href='javascript:show_detail
  ("watermelon")'  shape=rect
  coords="100,100,200,200" />
</map>
```

Jargon buster

An **image map** is an image that has 'hotspots' – areas within the image that when clicked can lead to different actions.

The map has areas that are defined by coordinates – the `coords` attribute sets the coordinates. Note that the four areas have coordinates that work within the size attributes set in the image tag. The image size is set at 200 × 200 pixels, and each area is defined to a quadrant. The four parameters in the `coords` attribute are left, top, right and bottom. Listing 16-4 shows the full page of code.

Listing 16-4 Using JavaScript with an image map

```
<html>
<head>
<title>Brilliant JavaScript</title>
```

16

Using an image map to control page visibility (cont.)

```
<style>
body {font-family:arial;font-
weight:bold;background-color:#eeeeff}
</style>
<script type="text/javascript">
function show_detail(fruit) {
   var d=  document.getElementsByTagName
   ("div");
   for (i=0;i<d.length;i++) {
     d[i].style.visibility="hidden";
   }
   document.getElementById(fruit).style.
   visibility="visible";
}
</script>
</head>
<body>
<br /><br />
<center>
<img src="fruit.jpg" width="200"
height="200" border="1" usemap="#4fruits">
</center>
<map name="4fruits">
  <area  href='javascript:show_detail
  ("apple")' shape=rect coords="1,1,100,100"
  />
  <area  href='javascript:show_detail
  ("strawberry")'  shape=rect
  coords="100,1,200,100" />
  <area  href='javascript:show_detail
  ("banana")' shape=rect
  coords="1,100,100,200" />
  <area  href='javascript:show_detail
  ("watermelon")' shape=rect
  coords="100,100,200,200" />
</map>
<div id="apple" style="visibility:hidden">
  Apples come in different colours
</div>
<div id="strawberry"
```

```
style="visibility:hidden">
    Strawberries are red and have seeds
</div>
<div id="banana" style="visibility:hidden">
    Bananas grow in a bunch
</div>
<div id="watermelon"
style="visibility:hidden">
    Watermelons are big, have seeds, and are
    watery
</div>
</body>
</html>
```

The typical use of an image map is such that when a hotspot is clicked, the `href` attribute is set to another URL (web page). In other words, click on a part of the map, and up comes a new page. In an image of fruit, you could expect that clicking on a strawberry would display a page about strawberries. Figure 16-5 shows the page as it first appears.

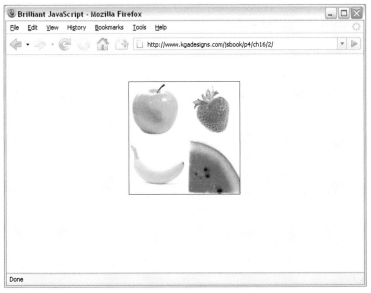

Figure 16-5 Click on a fruit

Using an image map to control page visibility (cont.)

In this image map variation, clicking on an image toggles the visibility of a `div` element. When the page loads, all `div` elements are set to hidden, as in this `div` about the apples:

```
<div id="apple" style="visibility:hidden">
  Apples come in different colours
</div>
```

When a fruit is clicked on, first all `div` elements are set to hidden, and then the one that was clicked is set to visible:

```
function show_detail(fruit) {
  var d=  document.getElementsByTagName
  ("div");
  for (i=0;i<d.length;i++) {
    d[i].style.visibility="hidden";
  }
  document.getElementById(fruit).style.
  visibility="visible";
}
```

Figure 16-6 shows the result of clicking on the banana. The banana `div` is visible, with an important banana fact.

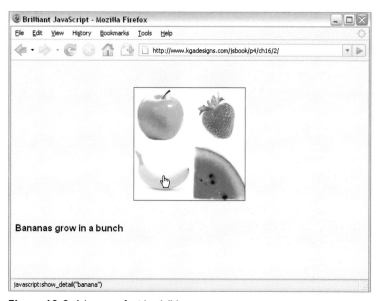

Figure 16-6 A banana fact is visible

JavaScript has an exception handling mechanism that is on a par with other modern languages. The `Try-Catch-Finally` block is the customary way to handle errors at this point of modern development.

The idea behind this is to gracefully handle an error so that (1) viewers won't be put off by a techno-babble scary message, and (2) the program keeps running.

Listing 16-5 shows how `Try-Catch` is implemented. The `Finally` part is optional.

Listing 16-5 Using a `Try-Catch` block to avoid program interruption

```html
<html>
<head>
<title>Brilliant JavaScript</title>
<style>
body {font-family:arial;font-
weight:bold;background-color:#eeeeff}
</style>
<script type="text/javascript">
function trycatch() {
    try   {
       docment.write("Good morning");
    }
    catch(e) {
       alert("An error occurred writing to
       the page");
    }
}
</script>
</head>
<body><center>
<input type="button" value="Click Me"
onclick="trycatch()" />
</center>
</body>
</html>
```

In Listing 16-5 is a line of bad code:

```
docment.write("Good morning");
```

Catching errors

16

Catching errors (cont.)

Instead of **document** the spelling is incorrect: **docment**. Looks similar but JavaScript is unforgiving. This creates an error. Without an error catch of some type, an unfriendly error message could appear, or nothing might appear. In the latter case, the error goes unnoticed, which could actually be worse than a message appearing.

To avoid this, a **try** statement is placed around the line. Thinking about it, you wouldn't put a **try** statement around code unless you expected that an error *could* occur. In this example the error is deliberate to show how the trap works:

```
try {
    docment.write("Good morning");
}
catch(e) {
    alert("An error occurred writing to
the page");
}
```

What is seen here is that the **try** statement is placed before the suspect code, and encases it by the placement of the curly braces, **{ }**. The **catch** statement is in place just after the **try** and does just what it says – it catches the error and does something with it. In this case an **alert** message is displayed.

The error will not be triggered until the button is clicked, because the error is inside the function that is called by the click. Figure 16-7 shows the displayed 'friendly' message.

The message text is based on the code in the catch statement. In other words, the programmer has decided what the error should say instead of letting the browser state the message, or not even display one at all.

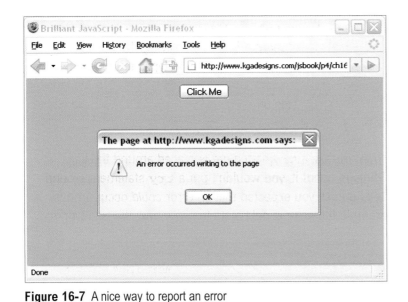

Figure 16-7 A nice way to report an error

Figure 16-8 shows the displayed message with a variation. Here, the actual error message itself, generated from the browser, is used, but incorporated with some human-speak.

Figure 16-8 Another nice way to report an error

Catching errors (cont.)

The one difference in the code is the line in the `catch` statement:

```
catch(e) {
    alert("This error has occurred: " +
    e.message);
}
```

Here the actual error message, derived from the message property of the error itself (`e.message`), is displayed with a prefix.

For your information

What about `finally`?

The `finally` statement is not always used, and when used needs to make sense. The `finally` statement will execute whether an error occurs or not. So if `finally` is left out, any statement after the `catch` statement will run anyway. Therefore using `finally` is most useful when there is an error, typically to provide an alternative or to reverse the action that created the error.

When you have been coding long enough, you realise that a lot of what you code is exactly like or similar to something you have coded before. Functions are the first in line to optimise repetitive code. When in a single application the same process is used many times, a function is used. Taking this a step further, there are functions that are used the same way in many applications.

When such functions are recognised they can be put in a separate file. This file acts as an external JavaScript file like that discussed in Chapter 1. In this case, the external file can and would be filled with many functions. This is a code library.

Figure 16-9 shows a web page that has content based on the use of three different functions. The first is not as obvious – it is the date showing at the top. The date was determined by a function.

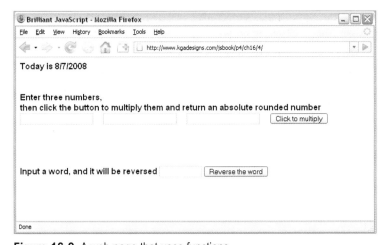

Figure 16-9 A web page that uses functions

Listing 16-6 shows the code of the web page in Figure 16-9.

Listing 16-6 External functions are called

```
<html>
<head>
<title>Brilliant JavaScript</title>
<style>
```

```
body {font-family:arial;font-weight:bold}
</style>
<script type="text/javascript"
src="library.js">
</script>
</head>
<body onload="return_date()">
<div id="thedate"></div>
<br /><br />
<form>
Enter three numbers,<br />
 then click the button to multiply them
and return an absolute rounded number
<br />
<input type="text" id="num1" size"6" />
   
<input type="text" id="num2" size"6" />
   
<input type="text" id="num3" size"6" />
   
<input type="button" value="Click to
multiply" onclick="multiply(num1, num2,
num3, 'answer1')"/>
<br /><br />
<div id="answer1"></div>
<br /><br /><br />
Input a word, and it will be reversed
<input type="text" id="word" size="10" />
<input type="button" value="Reverse the
word" onclick="reverse_string(word,
'reversed')"/>
<br /><br />
<div id="reversed"></div>
</form>
</body>
</html>
```

First, an external JavaScript file is referenced in:

```
<script type="text/javascript"
src="library.js">
</script>
```

Then further down the page some functions are called that are in the library file. For example, here is the call to the function that reverses a word:

```
onclick="reverse_string(word, 'reversed')"/>
```

Figure 16-10 shows the result of inputting numbers for the **multiply** function and of inputting a word for the **reverse_string** function.

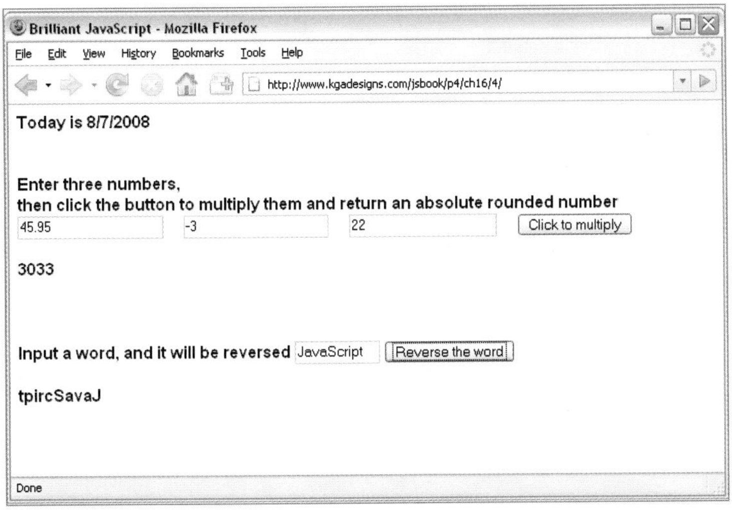

Figure 16-10 Answers returned from the external functions

Listing 16-7 shows the contents of the **library.js** file. In this file are multiple functions available for calling as needed.

Listing 16-7 Contents of the library file

```
function return_date() {
    var d=new Date();
    var month=new Array(12);
    month[0]="1";
    month[1]="2";
    month[2]="3";
    month[3]="4";
    month[4]="5";
    month[5]="6";
    month[6]="7";
```

```
      month[7]="8";
      month[8]="9";
      month[9]="10";
      month[10]="11";
      month[11]="12";
      fulldate=month[d.getMonth()] + "/" +
      d.getDate() + "/" + d.getFullYear();
      document.getElementById("thedate").
      innerHTML="Today is " + fulldate;
}
function square_root(number) {
      document.write(Math.sqrt(number));
}
function reverse_string(string,div) {
    string=string.value;
    var sLength=string.length;
    var reversed="";
    for (i=sLength;i>0;i—) {
      reversed=reversed + string.substr(i-
      1,1);
    }
    document.getElementById(div).inner
    HTML=reversed;
}
function multiply(num1, num2, num3, div) {
    answer=Math.abs(num1.value * num2.value *
    num3.value).toFixed(0);
    document.getElementById(div).innerHTML=
answer;
}
```

The three functions that are used in the web page of this example are in the library file. There is a fourth function, **square_root**, that is not used. However, this is the point of having a library. All your useful functions are kept in it and, based on the current application, the needed functions are called. Not all have to be used.

Jargon buster

Ajax – acronym for Asynchronous JavaScript And XML. There are two communication protocols – synchronous and asynchronous. Each moves data. Synchronous data exchange requires that the sender and the receiver are first in sync – established by coordinating on a few bits of preliminary information. Asychronous data is just sent, and the receiver can interpret it because in the asynchronous data there are start and stop bits.

Base62 – a numbering system. Numbers can be worked in any base. People work with base 10. Computers work with binary data (base 2), octal (8) and hex (16). A natural extension of doubling by 2 would arrive at 64. But 62 has no special meaning; it became a standard simply based on the alphanumeric association.

Cache – a temporary memory location.

Delimiter – synonymous with separator. Common delimiters are commas, semicolons, spaces and tabs, although any character can be used as long as it is used consistently throughout the larger string.

Elements – the individual items of an array.

Event – an event might be referred to as, for example, the `onclick` event, or just the click event; the terms are interchangeable.

Function – a discrete programming routine. Functions are called to run when needed. A perfect example is when you click a submit button to process an online form. Typically a validation routine will run, in this case upon the action of clicking the button.

Hard coding – embedding a value, as is, in the programming code, instead of having a variable represent the value. Hard coded values do not change.

Image map – an image that has 'hotspots' – areas within the image that when clicked on can lead to different actions.

Integer – a number without any decimal or fractional part, for example 5 is an integer but 5.02 is not an integer.

Obfuscation – making obscure or unclear.

Object – `Date ()` might be called a method but it's treated like an object. It is a method because it does something – it gets the current date and time. But it is instantiated like an object, and methods are used with it.

Onblur – the `onblur` event has nothing to do with something visual actually getting blurry. It is simply a complementary opposite of something that gets the focus.

Real number – a number that can have a decimal part, for example 5.02 is a real number, but plain old 5 is also a real number (think of it in terms of 5.00).

Select – a `select` is the proper HTML term for what is more commonly called a dropdown list; the terms are interchangeable.

String – synonymous with text. The words are interchangeable, but can also be referred to as a single entity – a text string.

XML – acronym for Extensible Markup Language. While that makes it sound as if it does something in the way a programming language would, XML is just a structured data storage standard. XML does not do anything. Instead, data in XML has methods applied to it.

Troubleshooting guide